Psycholinguistics

Thomas Scovel is a Professor in the
Department of English at San Francisco
State University.

D0964894

Published in this series:

Rod Ellis: *Second Language Acquisition*
Thomas Scovel: *Psycholinguistics*
Bernard Spolsky: *Sociolinguistics*
H.G. Widdowson: *Linguistics*
George Yule: *Pragmatics*

for Derick & Elizabeth

Contents

Preface

Purpose

What justification might there be for a series of introductions to language study? After all, linguistics is already well served with introductory texts: expositions and explanations which are comprehensive and authoritative and excellent in their way. Generally speaking, however, their way is the essentially academic one of providing a detailed initiation into the discipline of linguistics, and they tend to be lengthy and technical: appropriately so, given their purpose. But they can be quite daunting to the novice. There is also a need for a more general and gradual introduction to language: transitional texts which will ease people into an understanding of complex ideas. This series of introductions is designed to serve this need.

Their purpose, therefore, is not to supplant but to support the more academically oriented introductions to linguistics: to prepare the conceptual ground. They are based on the belief that it is an advantage to have a broad map of the terrain sketched out before one considers its more specific features on a smaller scale, a general context in reference to which the detail makes sense. It is sometimes the case that students are introduced to detail without it being made clear what it is a detail *of*. Clearly, a general understanding of ideas is not sufficient: there needs to be closer scrutiny. But equally, close scrutiny can be myopic and meaningless unless it is related to the larger view. Indeed it can be said that the precondition of more particular enquiry is an awareness of what, in general, the particulars are about. This series is designed to provide this large-scale view of different areas of language study. As such it can serve as preliminary to (and precondition for) the more specific and specialized enquiry which students of linguistics are required to undertake.

But the series is not only intended to be helpful to such students. There are many people who take an interest in language without being academically engaged in linguistics *per se*. Such people may recognize the importance of understanding language for their own lines of enquiry, or for their own practical purposes, or quite simply for making them aware of something which figures so centrally in their everyday lives. If linguistics has revealing and relevant things to say about language, then this should presumably not be a privileged revelation, but one accessible to people other than linguists. These books have been so designed as to accommodate these broader interests too: they are meant to be introductions to language more generally as well as to linguistics as a discipline.

Design

The books in the series are all cut to the same basic pattern. There are four parts: Survey, Readings, References, and Glossary.

Survey

This is a summary overview of the main features of the area of language study concerned: its scope and principles of enquiry, its basic concerns and key concepts. These are expressed and explained in ways which are intended to make them as accessible as possible to people who have no prior knowledge or expertise in the subject. The Survey is written to be readable and is uncluttered by the customary scholarly references. In this sense, it is simple. But it is not simplistic. Lack of specialist expertise does not imply an inability to understand or evaluate ideas. Ignorance means lack of knowledge, not lack of intelligence. The Survey, therefore, is meant to be challenging. It draws a map of the subject area in such a way as to stimulate thought, and to invite a critical participation in the exploration of ideas. This kind of conceptual cartography has its dangers of course: the selection of what is significant, and the manner of its representation, will not be to the liking of everybody, particularly not, perhaps, to some of those inside the discipline. But these surveys are written in the belief that there must be an alternative to a technical account on the one hand and an idiot's guide on the other if linguistics is to be made relevant to people in the wider world.

Readings

Some people will be content to read, and perhaps re-read, the summary Survey. Others will want to pursue the subject and so will use the Survey as the preliminary for more detailed study. The Readings provide the necessary transition. For here the reader is presented with texts extracted from the specialist literature. The purpose of these Readings is quite different from the Survey. It is to get readers to focus on the specifics of what is said and how it is said in these source texts. Questions are provided to further this purpose: they are designed to direct attention to points in each text, how they compare across texts, and how they deal with the issues discussed in the Survey. The idea is to give readers an initial familiarity with the more specialist idiom of the linguistics literature, where the issues might not be so readily accessible, and to encourage them into close critical reading.

References

One way of moving into more detailed study is through the Readings. Another is through the annotated References in the third section of each book. Here there is a selection of works (books and articles) for further reading. Accompanying comments indicate how these deal in more detail with the issues discussed in the different chapters of the Survey.

Glossary

Certain terms in the Survey appear in bold. These are terms used in a special or technical sense in the discipline. Their meanings are made clear in the discussion, but they are also explained in the Glossary at the end of each book. The Glossary is cross-referenced to the Survey, and therefore serves at the same time as an index. This enables readers to locate the term and what it signifies in the more general discussion, thereby, in effect, using the Survey as a summary work of reference.

Use

The series has been designed so as to be flexible in use. Each title is separate and self-contained, with only the basic format in common. The four sections of the format, as described here, can be drawn upon and combined in different ways, as required by the needs, or interests, of different readers. Some may be content with the Survey and the Glossary and may not want to follow up the suggested References. Some may not wish to venture into the Readings. Again, the Survey might be considered as appropriate preliminary reading for a course in applied linguistics or teacher education, and the Readings more appropriate for seminar discussion during the course. In short, the notion of an introduction will mean different things to different people, but in all cases the concern is to provide access to specialist knowledge and stimulate an awareness of its significance. This series as a whole has been designed to provide this access and promote this awareness in respect to different areas of language study.

H.G.WIDDOWSON

Author's Preface

One of the briefest and most memorable prayers in the Bible is found at the conclusion of Psalm 19:

Let the words of my mouth, and the meditation of my heart,
Be acceptable in thy sight,
O Lord, my strength, and my redeemer.

It may seem unusual to preface an introduction to a scientific discipline like psycholinguistics with this prayerful plea from the Book of Psalms, but words and thoughts (whether they are conceived in the heart, the mind, or even in the abdomen, as some cultures claim) are the central focus of this relatively new science. Further, their 'acceptability' depends very much on the norms and expectations of the language community in which they are conceived and shared. And because psycholinguistics is such a comprehensive discipline and embraces so many aspects of linguistic behavior, it then becomes obvious why I, as the author of this modest treatise on the topic, would begin with an invocation, not only to my maker, but to my reader! So obviously, there will be some sins of omission and commission, and for these limitations, I take no pride but do accept full responsibility, despite the help of many people who have deepened my understanding of the relationship between language and thought.

For several decades, I have enjoyed introducing psycholinguistics to students in many classes, both in the United States and in several countries around the globe, and in all of these courses, I have learned much from my students and from the authors of the many different texts we have used. I also have appreciated the insights shared by many professional friends, on my home campus, at academic conferences, and in the exchange of paper and electrons which makes modern communication so miraculously efficient. While trying to squeeze the writing of this book into a tight teaching schedule, I am, as always, grateful to my wife for tolerating my many sojourns into the study and for realizing that even an afternoon run into the nearby hills was not only good for the heart, but ultimately for the evolution of my scholarship as well.

Finally, I want to thank the good people at Oxford University Press for enlisting me as one of the authors for the Oxford Introductions to Language Study series. I was honored to be asked to participate, and I am grateful for their guidance, support, and most of all, for their patience, throughout the writing and production of this volume. My ultimate gratitude is reserved for the Series Editor, Henry Widdowson, who carefully helped shape my ideas, who painstakingly edited every page I produced, and who wisely and generously made my words and my thoughts more acceptable.

THOMAS SCOVEL
San Francisco, May 1997

Survey

1

Introduction

History is marked by the very human urge to explore and venture. From the earliest of recorded time, we have well-documented accounts of attempts to name and map the farthest reaches of the heavens, and as time has progressed over the centuries, humans have ventured to study the more immediate world—the flora, fauna, and terra firma closer to them. But it has only been very recently, within the last century or so, that we have dared to explore the most proximal portion of our universe—the human mind. It is no accident, of course, that the oldest science is astronomy and the newest is psychology, for distance not only prompts curiosity, it also fosters observational objectivity. Given the inordinate attention devoted to psychology in magazines, books, and television, it seems as if humanity is trying desperately to make up for lost time in its zeal to discover more about the human mind.

Why is psychology one of the newest sciences and why has the study of mind provoked so much recent attention? The answer to both questions appears to lie in the fact that of all the objects of inquiry in our universe, the human mind itself, the seat of all queries and inquiries, is the least amenable to objective study. So desperate are we for concrete, physical evidence that we frequently lapse into mistaking the mind for the brain. Emily Dickinson commits this error, but she can be forgiven, for she was a poet, not a neuropsychologist, and she wrote before the science of psychology even existed. Most importantly, her words tellingly capture the essential frustration of trying to fathom the most fathomless of abstractions, the human intellect.

The Brain is Wider

The brain is wider than the sky,
　For put them side by side,
The one the other will include
　With ease, and you beside.
The brain is deeper than the sky,
　For, hold them blue to blue,
The one the other will absorb
　As sponges, buckets do.
The brain is just the weight of God,
　For lift them, pound for pound,
And they will differ, if they do,
　As syllable from sound.

Substituting 'mind' for 'brain', we can share the poet's perception that the mind seems to encompass everything within our natural universe. Indeed, because it can also conceive of the supernatural, perhaps Dickinson is right; the mind is made, or is part and parcel of, the very image of God. The task of the scientist, however, is the exact opposite of the poet's. Rather than to expand, enlarge, and enliven the universe through creativity, the scientist must describe, delimit, and delineate through objectivity, and thus we return to the essential conundrum—without simplistically reducing it to the less than two kilograms of soft tissue in the cranium, how do we study the human mind? In the last fifty years or so, scientists interested in this most proximal piece of nature have carved out a field of inquiry which has begun to yield answers about the structure of the mind, and they have arrived at these answers, in part, by using evidence from a uniquely human possession—speech and language. The use of language and speech as a window to the nature and structure of the human mind is called **psycholinguistics**.

The vast majority of data and evidence quoted here will deal with language and speech; however, it is instructive to remember that this book is not an introduction to the study of language, linguistics, but rather an introduction to the **psychology of language** (a term often used as a synonym for psycholinguistics). Although sounds, words, and sentences will serve as examples throughout this book, they themselves are not the center of our attention; they will function instead as windows to the mind. And given the complexity of all languages and the collective complexity and individual complications of all human minds, it is understandable that linguistic data will only on occasion provide clear and transparent vistas of how the mind functions. More typically it will reveal only smudgy glimpses.

Like all disciplines, psycholinguistics has evolved into a conglomeration of sub-fields. However these divisions provide a means whereby a large body of information can be introduced in more digestible pieces. This book will examine research questions in four sub-fields: (1) how are language and speech *acquired*? (2) how are language and speech *produced*? (3) how are language and speech *comprehended*? and finally, (4) how are language and speech *lost*? One way to look at these questions is to view them as sets of pairs and picture them within the framework of a two-by-two matrix—a four-paned window, as it were, as set out in Figure 1.1.

	Diachronic	Synchronic
Synthesis	acquisition	production
Analysis	dissolution	comprehension

FIGURE 1.1

Viewed **diachronically**, over time, acquisition and dissolution are the beginning and the end of the story of speech in an individual human being. The former requires the skills of putting a new language together, while the latter reflects the unwanted and unintentional process of a language falling apart. Although these processes reflect the opposite ends of a continuum, they are not so disparate as they might initially appear. As the 'Seven ages of man' soliloquy from Shakespeare's *As You Like It* implies, the natural process of disintegration in old age may recapitulate the period of integration during infancy.

> Last scene of all,
> That ends this strange eventful history,
> Is second childishness, and mere oblivion,
> Sans teeth, sans eyes, sans taste, sans everything.
> *As You Like It* I. vii. 139

Seen **synchronically**, at any one point in time, however, production and comprehension can be considered as comparable psycholinguistic tasks; the former involves the synthesis of language structures while the latter involves their analysis. The production of language demands the synthetic talents of an imaginary mental chef, who selects the appropriate ingredients, weighs them carefully, and then stirs them together into a creative new dish. The comprehension of language, on the other hand, requires the analytic skills of a cognitive chemist, who takes whatever is served up and meticulously breaks it down into its individual compounds and elements in order to understand it completely.

These four major sub-fields of psycholinguistics collectively comprise the issues which will concern us in this book.

2
Acquisition: when I was a child, I spoke as a child

Children are a focus of attention and affection in all societies. The presence of an infant is a key to the hearts of strangers anywhere on the globe. 'What a cute smile', they murmur, immediately transfixed by the child's demeanor, 'What's her name?' they inquire. 'Does she speak yet?' Because of their universally unique status, small children evoke a certain sociolinguistic familiarity and directness not permissible with older children and adults. And if these encounters transpire in cross-cultural situations, for example when a couple are touring a foreign country with their young child, along with these typical expressions of affectionate attention come cries of amazement when the youngster is enticed or provoked into speaking its native tongue. There is a natural wonder when the strange and difficult sounds of a foreign language appear to pour effortlessly out of the mouths of mere babes.

It is no surprise, then, that the ability of children to pick up their mother tongue so quickly and seemingly so easily is the central concern of the first major sub-field of the psychology of language that we will review. **Developmental psycholinguistics** examines how speech emerges over time and how children go about constructing the complex structures of their mother tongue. The emergence of speech is not only an apt chronological stage to begin our reflections on the nature of the human mind, it is also the stage where we can glean the least complicated data. As Tennyson puts it, our first efforts at speech are not words but cries:

So runs my dream, but what am I?
    An infant crying in the night;
An infant crying for the light,
    And with no language but a cry.

So pervasive is the common perception that the crying of a baby conveys some significant linguistic communication, that the early Romans believed it was the gift of a specific spirit, Vigitanus, and even Plato observed that the very first communicative distinction is between comfort and discomfort. A common mistake of early students of developmental psycholinguistics was to assume that children had no language until they uttered their first word, usually about the time of their first birthday.

'... no language but a cry'

Over the past forty years, there has been an increasing amount of research into the linguistic capacity of infants, and it seems the more we study them the smarter they become. What we have learned about crying is that it is not only communicative, it is also a direct precursor to both *language* (human symbolic communication) and *speech* (spoken language). In a sense, crying, at least in the first few months, is a kind of language without speech, because the child communicates different types of discomfort without using normal speech sounds. As the infant matures, crying helps the child learn how to produce linguistic sounds, and so this earliest form of utterance is also a precursor to speech. During the first few weeks of a child's life, crying is largely an **autonomic** response to noxious stimuli, triggered by the autonomic nervous system as a primary reflex. In brief, this means that the crying response is hard-wired into the child, and crying is initially a spontaneous reaction, unaffected by intentional control from the voluntary nervous system, which eventually evolves as the mover and shaper of most human behavior. Even at this relatively primitive stage, however, crying is a direct preparation for a lifetime of vocal communication. As anyone can witness when observing a raucous infant in full voice, crying trains babies to time their breathing patterns so that eventually they learn how to play their lungs like bagpipes, with quick inhalations of air followed by long, slow exhalations to fuel their vocal cords with prolonged wailing. This skill of timed breathing is crucial for successful speech communication for the rest of the child's life, and it is a direct result of a baby's ability to learn to control the cries of birth.

Crying initially is completely **iconic;** there is a direct and transparent link between the physical sound and its communicative intent. For example the hungrier a baby becomes, the louder and the longer the crying. It also increases in pitch. The degree of discomfort is directly proportional to the intensity of the acoustic signal. But in the first month or two of the child's development, crying becomes more differentiated and more **symbolic.** This means that it is not directly related to the child's sense of discomfort; rather, the cries are subtly, indirectly, and almost randomly associated with its needs. As most mothers realize intuitively, and as recent studies have suggested, the baby may not cry to express discomfort or pain, but rather to elicit attention. So even at this rudimentary stage of linguistic evolution, there is a significant transformation from using sound as an iconic or direct reflection of an internal state to using it as a symbolic, indirect manifestation of increasingly complex internal feelings. Later, we will learn that this transition also represents a major difference between the communication found in most animals and the way humans use language.

Even at this earliest and most primitive stage of psycholinguistic development, we cannot simply pretend that the baby exists alone and evolves independently. Humans are born at an early stage of development in comparison with most mammals. Even when we are born after our natural full term of nine months, we are physically so weak and underdeveloped that we are completely dependent on our caretakers for several years. This forces and forges an enormous degree of early bonding and socialization. After several weeks of extensive interaction with its caretaker, the child starts to **coo,** making soft gurgling sounds, seemingly to express satisfaction. Crying and cooing affect, and are affected by, caretaker behavior. It is difficult to surmise whether the coos and gurgles of a just-fed baby reinforce the mother's contentment in caring it, or whether the mother's sounds of comfort when nurturing her baby reinforce the child's attempt to mimic the contentment it perceives. In a statistical study of the interactions between the sounds that ten Japanese mothers and their babies made when together, Nobuo Masataka showed that there was a clear similarity between the sounds made by mother and child which had emerged by the time the infants were only five months old. Most likely then, a baby's early vocalizations, and the constant responses of the caretaker, mutually reinforce each other. Obviously then, even these earliest attempts at communication underscore the importance of social interaction in the acquisition of human language.

This **cooing** stage emerges at about two months of age but is succeeded, when the child is about six months old, by a **babbling** stage. Babbling refers to the natural tendency of children of this age to burst out in strings of consonant–vowel syllable clusters, almost as a kind of vocalic play. Some psycholinguists distinguish between **marginal babbling,** an early stage similar to cooing where infants produce a few, and somewhat random, consonants, and **canonical babbling,** which usually emerges at around eight months, when the child's vocalizations narrow down to syllables that begin to approximate the syllables of the caretaker's language.

Interestingly enough, when infants begin to babble consonants at the canonical stage, they do not necessarily produce only the consonants of their mother tongue. That is, their earliest acquisition is not of the **segmental phonemes** (the individual consonants and vowels) that go to make up their native tongue. In fact, children seem to play with all sorts of segments at this stage, and frequently produce consonants that are found in other languages, not just the language by which they are surrounded. Hence we find the first of several psycholinguistic ironies. A six-month-old infant, raised by English speakers, may very well babble a sound that is not in her mother tongue—say the unaspirated /p/ sound in Spanish *pico* ('beak'), which sounds more similar to the English /b/ in 'by' than the aspirated English /p/ in 'pie.' But this same child, when trying to learn Spanish words twenty years later, may have great difficulty producing this same unaspirated Spanish /p/ sound she babbled with ease as a baby!

Since infants may babble vowels and consonants which are not part of their mother's native repertoire, babbling is not evidence that children are starting to acquiring the segmental sounds of their mother tongue. But recent psycholinguistic research supports earlier assumptions that children are beginning to learn the **suprasegmental** sounds of their mother tongue at this stage. The term suprasegmental refers to the musical pitch, rhythm, and stress which accompany the syllables we produce and which play such an important role in marking grammar, meaning, and intention. Eight-month-old babies reared in English-speaking families begin to babble with English-sounding melody; those of a similar age who are brought up in Chinese-speaking homes begin to babble with the tones and melodies of Chinese. Babbling is the first psycholinguistic stage where we have strong evidence that infants are influenced by all those many months of exposure to their mother tongue. Up to this stage, there is very little difference between the speech production of a normal child and that of a baby born profoundly deaf. Both infants will progress through the crying and cooing stages with little overt manifestation of the significant difference between them in hearing ability. However, as the babbling stage begins, a half a year into life, the lack of suprasegmental accuracy in the babbling of a deaf baby is often the first overt signal of the child's disability.

First words

After crying, cooing, and babbling, we come to the culmination of a child's early language development—the first word. A child crosses this linguistic Rubicon at about one year old, although there is a wide range of latitude as to when the first word emerges and as to what constitutes a 'word'. For one thing, it seems that children often use **idiomorphs**, words they invent when they first catch on to the magical notion that certain sounds have a unique reference. For example, one psycholinguist recorded that when his daughter was about one year old, she came up with 'ka ka' as the word for 'milk'. But just as frequently, youngsters begin to learn the vocabulary of their mother tongue straight away. A survey of the words children first learn to say shows that they tend to be those which refer to prominent, everyday objects, and usually things that can be manipulated by the child. Thus, 'mama' and 'dada' (of course), and 'doggie', 'kitty', but also 'milk', 'cookie', and 'sock'. Even at this most rudimentary stage of vocabulary development, we can see evidence for what Piaget calls **egocentric speech**. Children, quite naturally, want to talk about what surrounds them; at life's beginnings, they are the center of their universe. If the child cannot manipulate the object during this early period of physical development, it does not appear to be worth naming. Parents spend a lot of time putting diapers on and taking them off their one-year-olds, but because babies themselves (quite fortunately!) don't handle them, 'diapers' or 'nappies' do not become part of a child's early linguistic repertoire.

Parents fuss a great deal over their child's first word; this, and the first step, rank as singular benchmarks of maturation. The first cry, the first coo, or the first babble is often ignored or unrecognized, but the first substantive evidence of vocabulary acquisition, even if indistinguishable from a controlled burp to outsiders, is often duly recorded and dated by proud parents. Just as the first steps are symbolic of the evolution of man from ape-like animal to biped, the first few words, whether idiomorphs or words from the parent's native language, demonstrate to the mother and father that their child has successfully made the transition from an iconic creature to a symbolic human being.

The Miracle Worker, the compelling drama about the early life of Helen Keller, saves this marvelous moment for its powerful conclusion. Annie Sullivan, the teacher hired to transform the blind and deaf, asocial and non-communicative young Helen, has been laboring throughout the play to get Helen to communicate by finger spelling, but now, with Annie's contract almost up, all seems hopeless. Helen remains entrapped in an iconic world without speech or language. But as they stand in the well-house, next to the water pump, where Annie has led Helen for her daily chore of filling the pitcher for dinner, the water spills accidentally on Helen's hands and the miracle unfolds. Helen seizes Annie's hand and finger-spells what Annie has written so many times on Helen's hand, apparently without success. W-A-T-E-R. From this moment on, words cascade onto Helen's fingers like the water which is accidentally spilt at the well; and from this moment comes an explosion of linguistic learning, so that Helen is eventually able to write about the experience in her own words.

That living word awakened my soul, gave it light, hope, joy, set it free ... I left the well-house eager to learn. Everything had a name, and each name gave birth to a new thought.

(from Helen Keller. 1903. *The Story of My Life*. Doubleday, page 44)

More remarkable than the drama, and the actual biographical anecdote it depicts, is that most of us have experienced a similar moment when, at about the age of one, we too suddenly recognized 'the mystic harmony, linking sense to sound and sight', and entered the sentient and symbolic world of human communication. Once the first few words are acquired, there is an exponential growth in vocabulary development, which only begins to taper at about the age of six, when, by some estimates, the average child has a recognition vocabulary of about 14,000 words. It is no wonder then that parents are excited by their child's first word: it represents a step into symbolic communication, and it signifies the start of the rapid vocabulary growth with which thoughts, feelings, and perceptions, as well as other areas of linguistic development, are framed.

The birth of grammar

Even well over a century ago, parents noticed that their children seemed to use single words as sentences. In 1877 Charles Darwin, for example, recorded in the journal that he kept on his son's acquisition of language that the single word 'milk' could sometimes be a statement or a request, or, if his son had accidentally dropped his glass, an exclamation. This use of single words as skeletal sentences is referred to as the **holophrastic** stage, and though there is some debate about its verifiability, most psycholinguists believe that the intonational, gestural, and contextual clues which accompany holophrases make it clear that children are using single-word sentences, exactly as adults often do in conversation. 'Milk?' is often used as the truncated form of 'Do you have any milk?' but, given the appropriate context, 'Milk!' is just as obviously an abbreviated version of 'I'd like some milk'. Recall that from the very beginning, infants are reared and nurtured in a world where virtually all communication evolves through intimate social interaction, and so it is entirely plausible that a child's earliest form of grammar should manifest itself in the same highly contextualized holophrastic utterances which adults use when conversing with each other in familiar social settings. Holophrastic speech is the bridge which transports the child from the primitive land of cries, words, and names across into the brave new world of phrases, clauses, and sentences.

Of all the areas investigated by developmental psycholinguists, the acquisition of grammar has been studied the most intensively. Much of this can be related to the development of **Transformational-Generative (TG) grammar**, the most influential school of linguistics to affect the study of language over the past four decades. Although TG grammar has evolved and devolved into many different sub-schools, it has always been involved most centrally with the study of sentences. Another reason why people investigating child first language acquisition are inclined to focus on the attempts of children to acquire grammar is that the data is easy to obtain. Unlike the tape recordings of cooing, babbling, and burping babies, where the acoustic signals are fuzzy and the gathering of data a laborious and indeterminate task, the gleaning of information on how children create sentences is manageable, discrete, and can be done while caring for the child. No wonder that so many studies are done on the acquisition of grammar by toddlers as they converse with their parent/linguist parent at home. The transcripts recorded often reveal the amazing ability of youngsters to acquire their mother tongue fluently and, at the same time, create novel expressions.

Father/Linguist (Supervising daughter getting dressed): 'I think you've got your underpants on backwards.'
Daughter (Age 3 [yrs] 9 [months]): 'Yes, I think so.'
Father/Linguist: 'You'd better take them off and put them on frontwards.'
Daughter (Taking them off and turning them around): 'Is this the *rightwards*?'

(from Peter Reich. 1986. *Language Development*. Prentice-Hall, page 142)

Even at an earlier age, a child's acquisition of syntax displays a subtle but definitive understanding of universal properties of human language. Roger Brown and his colleagues, in the first, elaborate chronology of how children acquire English grammar, published in 1973, demonstrated that children progress through different **stages** of grammatical development, measured largely by the average number of words occurring per utterance. Although individuals differ, especially at very young ages, in the speed with which they move from one stage to another, all children begin to create sentences after the holophrastic stage, first with two words, and subsequently with more. The many studies conducted of the early two-word stage reveal that, even within these limitations, children demonstrate a surprising amount of grammatical precocity. They do not randomly rotate words between first and second position, for example; certain words (**pivots**) tend to be used initially or finally, and other words then can be used to fill in the slot either after or before these so-called pivots. The order of the words in these two-word utterances tends to follow the normal word order of the expanded version used by adults in longer sentences, which indicates that children are already sensitive to the word order of their mother tongue. Finally, it is quite rare for youngsters to repeat the same word twice in forming their little sentences; children are parsimonious with their language and make each word count.

A telling indication of just how much children have acquired by the time they are approximately two years old, and have begun to use two-word sentences consistently, is to contrast examples of their grammar with the output collected from one of the most prominent experiments to teach a human language to a chimpanzee. The chimp examples below come from a project which attempted to improve upon previous attempts to teach a form of human sign language (**American Sign Language** or **ASL**) to young chimpanzees. ASL has become a popular human language to teach to these animals because, due to the anatomical differences between human and simian vocal tracts, chimps cannot make the sounds of a human language. In this project, the researchers' young pupil was 'Nim Chimsky', named, of course, after the father of TG grammar, Noam Chomsky. The examples below contrast utterances by a two-year old human child with Nim's longest attempts to sign in ASL. Even though this comparison is already skewed in Nim's favour—two-word utterances by the child are contrasted with four-word phrases by the chimp—it is clear that in terms of conveying meaning, the child's language is far more developed.

Two-word utterances by a human child
(from M. D. S. Braine. 1963. The ontogeny of English phrase structure: The first phrase. *Language* 39:1–13)

it ball	see ball	get ball	there ball	want baby
it doll	see doll	get doll	there doll	want car
it checker	see Steve	get Betty	there momma	want do
it daddy			there doggie	want get
it boy			there book	want up

Four-word phrases in ASL by a chimp
(from H. S. Terrance. 1979. *Nim: A Chimpanzee Who Learned Sign Language.* Washington Square Press, page 319)

(1) eat drink eat drink   (6) grape eat Nim eat
(2) banana Nim banana Nim   (7) banana eat me Nim
(3) eat Nim eat Nim   (8) banana me eat banana
(4) Nim eat Nim eat   (9) play me Nim play
(5) banana me Nim me   (10) drink Nim drink Nim

Even in this sparse amount of data, there are obvious differences in performance. The child displays great lexical diversity (19 items): the chimp seems confined to a small stock of words (7 items). The child displays very little repetition. The chimp seems to find it impossible to sign a single sentence without referring to either 'Nim' or 'banana'. The child appears to have a sense of syntax: a two-word sequence is introduced by a pivot word like 'it' or 'want', which is followed by a slot filled by a wide variety of lexical items. The chimp, on the other hand, is a prolific producer of permutations: he can cleverly churn out random sequences of signs, but there are no fixed pivot words around which predictable slots can occur. In sum, the child's output can be symbolized by a simple set of **phrase structure rules**, grammatical rules which demonstrate that a series of words form a structured phrase or clause and are not simply a list of unconnected items. The child's sequences appear to be more like words in a sentence. The chimp's sequences, on the other hand, seem to be much less like sentences and more like a grocery list. Thus they are much more difficult to describe by rules.

Notice that the child has a simple set of rules which are very powerful; they generate a large number of diverse utterances. Each rule is a logical linguistic extension of the previous rule. This capacity to generate new utterances has long been observed as an essential and universal characteristic of human language. In the eighteenth century, the German philosopher Leibnitz observed that 'human language uses finite resources to create infinite utterances', and two centuries later Chomsky founded the TG school of grammar on the same insight. Note too that the child's rules are elegant and simple, the two criteria most valued by grammarians, logicians, and theoretical mathematicians.

In contrast, the chimp's 'rule system', if we can be so generous as to call it such, is not nearly so tidy; indeed, these 'rules', like the actual data they attempt to reflect, are an ungainly sequence of random collocations. Nim's 'grammar', if it can be called a grammar, is unable to provide rules which can be used to describe many different sentences.

In comparing these two sets of data, we are led to the inescapable conclusion that even at a very young age, before they have any conscious awareness of the difference between parts of speech such as nouns and verbs, young humans very rapidly acquire the notion that words do not combine randomly but follow a systematic pattern of permissible sequences. Even at the stage when they are still producing two-word utterances, this system allows young children to generate a wide range of linguistic permutations. Chimps, on the other hand, do not appear to have even an inkling of any pattern or system, but randomly throw signs together in a haphazard fashion. At best, Nim's 'grammar' seems to tell him something like 'throw any four signs together from any category, and the nice man will give me a banana or a grape!'

Evidence for innateness

The example we have just reviewed is only one measure of the weight of evidence for **innateness**, which is the belief most psycholinguists now hold that the acquisition of human language is not based solely on the external influence of a child's environment. If linguistic stimuli from a child's or chimp's surroundings were indeed solely responsible for language acquisition, we would not expect such a glaring discrepancy between the performance of these two primate species. In fact, we might even expect Nim to be the better of the two performers because he was constantly bombarded with signs and was continually rewarded and reinforced whenever he attempted to use them to communicate with his handlers. And although human children also receive an enormous amount of linguistic input on any given day, they are infrequently rewarded just for speaking up, indeed they are sometimes encouraged to be 'seen but not heard'. There are even cultures (for example some of the Native American tribes of Arizona and New Mexico) which discourage young children from engaging adults in prolonged conversation. This kind of argument led Chomsky and a whole generation of developmental psycholinguists to claim that a sizeable part of early linguistic learning comes from an innately specified language ability in human beings. In other words, learning your mother tongue is a very different enterprise from learning to swim or learning to play the piano.

No one would argue, not even the most radical rationalist, that humans have innate areas of their brain genetically programmed to help them swim the back stroke, or play a tune on the piano. Environmental conditioning is crucial for these and many other human activities, and among the plethora of arguments in support of this fact is the simple observation that huge numbers of people never learn to swim or to play the piano at all, yet it is exceedingly rare, as we shall discover in Chapter 5, to stumble across anyone who has never learned to speak. Chomsky has argued that just as humans have some kind of genetically determined ability to 'learn' to stand upright or to walk, so too do they possess an **LAD**, a '**Language Acquisition Device**' (now replaced with the more linguistically accurate **UG** or '**Universal Grammar**'). Chomsky's position is accepted by a great many contemporary psycholinguists and is most articulately and assiduously defended in Steven Pinker's popular book, *The Language Instinct*. In summary, to return to humans and chimps, most psycholinguists agree that an ape like Nim will never be able to ape his human namesake, nor any one of us, without the human DNA molecules that account for so much of our collective behavior and our unique humanity.

Childish creativity

There is another way in which child language acquisition is relatively independent from environmental influences, despite the distinct control that the latter exercise on the course of our first language development. Obviously, a child's linguistic surroundings determine its mother tongue: children raised in Shandong, China, grow up speaking Mandarin; children raised in Bedfordshire, England, grow up as native speakers of English; and children, like your author, who grow up in Shandong but are reared by native speakers of English, usually acquire bilingual proficiency in both of these tongues. But despite the obvious impact the environment has on the choice and general direction of mother-tongue learning, children are prone to come up with all kinds of words and expressions which they have never heard in their mono- or bilingual environments. Children are creative wordsmiths, as evidenced in the following exchange between a friend and her two-year-old.

Daughter: Somebody's at the door.
Mother: There's nobody at the door.
Daughter: There's *yesbody* at the door.

(from P. Reich. 1986. *Language Development*. Prentice-Hall, page 142)

From about two to four, children produce all kinds of expressions like this which they have never, or rarely, heard in their environment, but which they create on their own in their attempts to construct, or reconstruct, their mother tongue. Common at this age are regular plurals for irregular ones (*mans, knifes, sheeps*), regular past-tense endings for irregular verbs (*goed, singed, eated*), and even 'double tensing' when children seem to be caught in transition between recognizing an irregular verb and yet reluctant to jettison the regular past-tense ending that they have acquired. This kind of **tuning**, to use a term to describe one type of cognitive processing, usually shows that the child has progressed to a slightly more advanced linguistic stage of language development ('Yesterday, we *wented* to Grandma's.'). Overgeneralizations like these are very common in the mother tongue learning of young children and are, perhaps mistakenly, referred to as 'false' analogies. One could make a convincing case that it is not the child who is in error but the language, since it fails to adhere to the symmetry of its own grammatical patterning. This process of **creative construction** is yet another example of the relative autonomy of the child's developing linguistic system in relation to the adult version of the language. Children are not chimps, and are definitely not parrots or tape recorders. They are a bit more like well-programmed computers, who make creative, but often inaccurate guesses about the rules and patterns of the language they are acquiring.

Even at this early age, children can sometimes display a profound understanding of the syntactic machinery of their mother tongue. There is some irony in the fact that, through their creative syntax, they reveal linguistic rules or patterns which might well have escaped the grammatical ken of their highly educated parents. One three-year-old child, upon spying a family friend approaching for dinner, exclaimed: '*There Carlos is!*' It took considerable effort on the father's part to figure out why this sentence was ungrammatical, but why it also sounded almost acceptable. The child was probably overgeneralizing from Patterns A and B to form the close-but-not-perfect C (marked with an asterisk * to indicate its ungrammaticality).

Pattern A:	There's Carlos!	[There's/Here's + Noun]
Pattern B:	There he is!	[There/Here Pronoun + is]
Pattern C:	*There Carlos is!	[There/Here + Noun + is]

Readers afflicted with a pathological addiction to grammar might want to consider how complex this particular paradigm really is, as well as how clever a linguistic puzzle solver this observant child had become.

Sometimes, children's creative constructions reflect their apparently inborn sensitivity to the syntactic structures of the language they are acquiring. Consider the following two examples of the creation of two-word verbs using *up* by two different five-year-olds.

A.K.:   Ben's hicking up. He's hicking up.
Adult: What?
A.K.:   He's got the hiccups.

(from S. A. Kuczaj II. 1978. Why do children fail to over-
generalize the progressive inflection? *Journal of Child
Language* 5: 167:710)

Father: Don't interrupt.
Child: Daddy, you're interring up!

(from C. Hockett. 1968. *The State of the Art*. Mouton,
page 115)

There is nothing wrong with the hearing of these two children.
In the first example, *hiccup* and '*hick up*' are phonologically
indistinguishable. In the second, given the fact that final consonant clusters in English (as in the cluster /pt/ of 'interrupt'), especially when they are voiceless, are usually not fully pronounced,
the difference between the final syllable of '*inter up*' vs. '*interrupt*'
would be consistently difficult to perceive in normal conversation, even for an adult. So the children's 'errors', if we wish to
label them such, are not mistakes of the ear, and since, of course,
these children have not yet learned to read, neither are they slips
of the eye. Rather, they are another example of how children cre-
atively construct their grammars based on what they have learned
and on what they can plausibly assume. Indeed, their assumption
about the structure of English in these examples appears to
reveal an uncanny awareness of a growing grammatical trend.
Compared to most other languages in the world, including its
cousins from Europe to South Asia, contemporary English has
become very much a 'prepositional' language, and one indication
of this tendency is the growing profusion of 'two-word' verbs—
verbs plus prepositions such as *turn on* or *look over*. The point is
that children are not only active and creative participants in the
acquisition of their mother tongue; even their 'errors' often indicate that they are remarkably sensitive to the subtle but inherent
grammatical characteristics of the language they are learning.

Stages of linguistic development

The study of child first language acquisition has now become an autonomous and growing discipline with its own texts, journals, and national and international conferences. It is difficult to present a concise summary of such a massive amount of research, even limiting our curiosity to just the acquisition of English as a mother tongue. Another large and equally burgeoning subdiscipline of developmental psycholinguistics is the area of bilingualism and its ancillary—and often politically controversial—branch devoted to bilingual education. Adding to the scope of this body of knowledge is the extension of first language acquisition research to older ages of childhood in order to investigate what kinds of complex linguistic structure are acquired by elementary school-aged children and, equally important, what possible age constraints on mother-tongue learning might reveal themselves when children turn into teenagers. For example, the emergence of 'foreign accents' in the speech of bilingual children at about the age of twelve suggests to some psycholinguists that there exists a **critical period** for first language learning which is biologically determined. To conclude this brief summary of an ever-expanding field, let us take a look at one universal and pervasive phenomenon that has been discovered at all ages of child language learning, with virtually every type of linguistic structure, and in all of the scores of world languages where child development has been intensively investigated. What most typifies first language acquisition is the fact that it invariably occurs in stages.

We must preface this brief description of the stages of language acquisition with the admission that there is and always will be individual differentiation. In all biological populations, there are always exceptions which fall on either side of the normal structure or behavior that defines a particular species, and this individuality is very conspicuous among *Homo Sapiens*. In one of the earliest pieces of research on the acquisition of a mother tongue by several child subjects, Roger Brown discovered that there was a glaring difference in the **rate** of language learning among the three children that he and his co-workers researched over a period of several years. Indeed, at about three years of age, one of the three children studied was linguistically already a year ahead of the other two. This should not be surprising, given the differences which exist in all animal species, and the great diversity of genetic and early environmental backgrounds that are found in even the most seemingly homogenous human populations. This differentiation can be seen in the supernormal performances of those rare children who burst forth from their peers with a genius for language, music, art, or sport. Consequently, these prodigies are becoming increasingly studied by psychologists because of their very individuality. But in spite of these individual differences, perhaps the most consistent finding in all of developmental psycholinguistics has been that there are universal stages of language learning. All children, no matter how rapid or how pedestrian their rate of acquisition, proceed systematically through the same learning stages for any particular linguistic structure.

An early example of this is found in the work of Brown's colleagues, Edward Klima and Ursula Bellugi, who proved that children learning English produce two different types of WH questions before they eventually come up with the correct adult version. They identified three distinct stages.

Stage 1
(use of WH word but no auxiliary verb employed)
What Daddy doing?
Why you laughing?
Where Mommy go?

Stage 2
(use of WH word and auxiliary verb after subject)
Where she will go?
Why Doggy can't see?
Why you don't know?

Stage 3
(use of WH word and auxiliary verb before subject)
Where will she go?
Why can't Doggy see?
Why don't you know?

(E.S. Klima and U. Bellugi. 1966 'Syntactic regularities in the speech of children' in J. Lyons and R.J. Wales (eds.): *Psycholinguistic Papers*. University of Edinburgh Press. Pages 183–208)

All children begin with Stage 1 utterances before proceeding to Stage 2 examples several months later. Eventually they end up with the linguistically appropriate target examples at Stage 3. No matter how precocious the children are, that is, no matter how fast their rate of progress through these stages, they do not skip over any of them; no child goes from Stage 1 immediately to Stage 3 without at least some examples of Stage 2 structures. Rates vary; stages don't.

Another example of developmental stages is seen in the acquisition of English negatives, again originally described by Brown and his colleagues in their study of the language learning of three young children. Brown divided their grammatical development into periods of '**Mean Length of Utterances**' (**MLU**s), showing that as the children progressed in the acquisition of their mother tongue, their MLUs grew from a minimum of about two words to about four. Recall that even when children are not yet two years old and are just beginning to string two words together, they seem to notice that words are not simply piled on top of one another like bricks. Certain words act as mortar and seem to hold words together in a certain order. It is this sensitivity to word choice and structure that allows children to create grammatical sentences, and it is the lack of this syntactic sense that appears to prevent chimps from creating sequences resembling human language. One example of young children's acquisition sensitivity to syntax is in the way they learn negation in English. Note how the primitive negatives found in Stage 1 (with an MLU of 1.75 words) eventually evolve into the adult-like forms of Stage 3 (where the MLUs are from 3.5 to 4 words).

Stage 1
(use of NO at the start of the sentence)
No the sun shining.
No Mary do it.

Stage 2
(use of NO inside the sentence but no auxiliary or BE verb)
There no rabbits.
I no taste it.

Stage 3
(use of NOT with appropriate abbreviation of auxiliary or BE)
Penny didn't laugh.
It's not raining.

(E.S. Klima and U. Bellugi. 1966 'Syntactic regularities in the speech of children' in J. Lyons and R.J. Wales (eds.): *Psycholinguistic Papers*. University of Edinburgh Press. Pages 183–208)

There may be some argument over the exact number of stages for a given structure; some researchers have suggested that there are four, not three, stages represented in the two grammatical examples illustrated here. However, starting with these examples taken from Brown's early fieldwork, there has been continual confirmation of the existence of sequential staging for many of the grammatical patterns acquired by children learning their first language, and of the finding that all children proceed immutably from one stage to the next. One especially insightful development in this research on acquisition stages has been the discovery that similar stages and staging is found in adult second language learning. Research pursued by applied linguists for several decades demonstrates that, like little children, adolescent and adult foreign language learners also differ a great deal in their *rate* of language acquisition but not in the *stages* through which they progress. This finding has several implications, but one of the most obvious is the possibility that the process of language acquisition is a common psychological challenge for both the young, maturing child, and the older, experienced adult. When it comes to the human mind, age differences tend to evaporate, and we witness one common cognitive process when the minds of either youngsters or their older counterparts are confronted with a similar task, for example the tremendous challenge of picking up a completely new system of symbolic communication—in other words, learning a language.

The inquiring and acquiring mind is the common denominator for all areas of psycholinguistics and is, perhaps, an apt topic with which to conclude this discussion of first language acquisition and to begin to contemplate language production.

3
Production: putting words in one's mouth

We are quick to recognize the exceptional precocity of talented writers, artists, or athletes, but we often fail to appreciate the gifts underlying so many of our everyday activities. It is only through loss or injury that we suddenly realize how much we take them for granted. The skill involved in such a literally pedestrian activity as walking down a flight of stairs is immediately recognized after one has sprained an ankle. It is only then that we begin to appreciate the marvelous manner in which the visual input from our eyes and the tactile information from our feet transmit complementary information to our brain's sensory cortex. There it is immediately synthesized and fed to corresponding areas of the motor cortex which, in turn, feeds the cerebellum, the part of the brain devoted to the programming, timing, and coordination of all voluntary muscular movements. From the cerebellum radiate hundreds of simultaneous messages along the nerve pathways which go to the appropriate muscles involved in the head and neck (to focus the face and eyes downward toward the stairwell), in the back (to keep the posture erect and tilted slightly backward to compensate for the downward motion of the body), in the arms and hands (to slide down the banister for continual support and feedback), in the legs (to maintain a lifting and dropping motion quite different from normal walking), and in the feet (to angle the foot in just the right manner so that the ball of the foot catches the stair). Even this elaborate description is a gross oversimplification of the neurosensory and neuromuscular processes that are involved at any single moment of a descent down a staircase. But all of this is taken for granted and considered uninteresting, until we stumble and injure ourselves. Loss of what we consider the simple and common gives us renewed appreciation of life's uncommon complexity.

The production of speech is neurologically and psychologically far more complicated than negotiating a flight of stairs, but its intricacy also goes unappreciated until we suffer some linguistic disability or commit a slip of the tongue. In daily conversations, we remain generally unaware of the complexity of our achievement. Again, it is only through disability that our marvelous ability is made manifest.

We have already seen in the previous chapter that psycholinguists tend to divide linguistic phenomena into stages. One of the most influential psycholinguistic models for speech production, developed by Levelt, views it as a linear progression of four successive stages: (1) **conceptualization**, (2) **formulation**, (3) **articulation**, and (4) **self-monitoring**. We will look at each of these in turn, not forgetting that viewing speech phenomena as a step-by-step sequential process is only one way of investigating production. Alternative approaches exist; for example, characterizing the production of speech as a holistic activity where several simultaneous and parallel activities are taking place to create the utterances we intend to produce.

Conceptualization

Where does the very beginning of any spoken utterance come from? What sparks speech? These are difficult questions to answer, partly because we still don't know enough about how language is produced, but partly because they deal with mental abstractions so vague that they elude empirical investigation. The American psycholinguist David McNeill, however, has gone on record with an interesting mentalistic account of how speech is first conceptualized in the human mind. His theory is that primitive linguistic concepts are formed as two concurrent and parallel modes of thought. These are **syntactic thinking**, which spawns the sequence of words which we typically think of when we talk about how language is initiated, and **imagistic thinking**, which creates a more holistic and visual mode of communication. The former is segmented and linear and creates the strings of syllables, words, phrases, and sentences that together make up speech.

The latter is global and synthetic and tends to develop the gestures which we naturally use to punctuate and illustrate our conversations.

McNeill's claim, that syntactic thought and imagistic thought collaborate to conceptualize conversation, is quite convincingly demonstrated by the way in which speech utterances and ordinary gestures seem to be tied and timed together in any conversation. Consider the following very simple example. Two people are holding a short discussion over the whereabouts of a lost object. Visualize in your mind how they gesture as they interact in the following two dialogues. You might even try reading these aloud, acting out Person B's role by pointing at the appropriate moment.

First dialogue
Person A: Where's my briefcase?
Person B: *There's* your briefcase!
Person B points to the briefcase the same moment he says *There's*.

Second dialogue
Person A: Where's my coat and briefcase?
Person B: There's your *briefcase*!
Person B points to the briefcase the same moment he says *briefcase*.

What are the very first things that are going through Person B's mind when she is responding to Person A's questions in these two dialogues? Of course we cannot be too mentalistic and pretend we know what B is thinking. After all, we are often unsure of what we are thinking ourselves when we think about what we think, if we think about thinking at all. This is the problem with mentalism. But McNeill offers some plausible evidence for this bimodal view of how speech is produced. It seems likely that after B hears A's query in the first example, her syntactic thought might generate something that begins with the demonstrative, 'there' while, simultaneously, her imagistic thought might be of someone pointing toward an object, in this case, a briefcase. Evidence that these two modes are operating concurrently at the conceptualization stage is found in the simultaneous timing of the pointing gestures with the stressed words in each of these two scenes. In the first dialogue, B points to the briefcase (manifesting the imagistic part of her attempt to communicate) just as she stresses the word 'there' in her speech (illustrating the syntactic component of her communicative intent). Again, in the second dialogue, we see the synchrony of image and speech; at the end of the phrase B points to the briefcase just as she stresses the word in her articulation. If you read this last example out loud, you will also note a slight change in B's intonation—the voice trails off a bit as if to say 'There's your *briefcase* ...' Were B suddenly to spot the coat, she could continue with 'and there's your *coat*', with a more decisive, falling intonation on 'coat' and, of course, another pointing gesture to show A where his coat was located.

Appealing as McNeill's hypothesis might appear, and convincing as these examples might be, it is difficult to use his model to explain this first stage of production. For one thing, his attempts to describe how imagistic and syntactic thought are initially conceptualized are unclear. For another, the illustrations he uses to describe how gestures synchronize with important syntactic breaks in spoken language are difficult to follow. Perhaps this form of research, like studies of American Sign Language, can only be adequately illustrated by a videotape and not by drawings.

Levelt's initial stage of conceptualization seems justified. After all, speech does not start from nothing, and if it does not start with concepts, how else could it possibly begin? At the same time, we realize how difficult it is to actually define this stage in non-mentalistic terms, and despite the plausibility of McNeill's binary model of language and gestures being birthed together, like twins, it is difficult to muster any hard evidence to support this, or any other theory for the embryonic development of speech. Although we know very little about how speech is initiated at this first stage of conceptualization, we have psycholinguistic evidence to help us understand the successive stages of production, so it is easier for us to describe and to understand Levelt's second stage, formulation.

Formulation

Introduction

We have seen that the initial stage of conceptualization is so far removed from the words we actually speak and write that it is difficult to delineate this phase of production. But at the second stage of speech production, formulation, we move close enough to the eventual output of the process to allow us to be more precise in our terminology and more convincing in our use of empirical data. Conceptualization is hard to conceptualize, but formulation is much easier to formulate. Well over three decades ago, the psychologist Karl Lashley published one of the first attempts to account for the way speakers sequence strings of sounds, words, and phrases together so rapidly and accurately, and his essay was influential enough to be included in the first book ever published in English which focused exclusively on the then very new field of the psychology of language. His essay was first presented as an oral address, and it is intriguing to see how Lashley organized it to demonstrate some of the very concepts about speech production which he was writing about. For example, he talked about how common it is to commit spelling errors when one is typing, and he mentioned how he misspelled 'wrapid' with a w, while typing 'rapid writing', most probably because as he was about to type 'rapid', he anticipated the 'silent w' in the following word. These slips of the tongue, or pen, or computer keyboard, are of keen interest to us in this chapter on production. A moment later in his talk, to illustrate several of the themes that were central to his presentation, Lashley gave the following utterance as an example of how we comprehend spoken sentences.

Rapid righting with his uninjured hand saved from loss the contents of the capsized canoe.

Remember that this sentence was *heard*, not seen, so having been primed by the earlier phrase 'rapid writing', it was natural for the audience to hear 'Rapid *writing* with his uninjured hand!' Of course, like all native speakers of any language, the listeners were able to readjust their comprehension of this sentence. After they recognized they had initially wandered down the wrong garden path of comprehension, they were forced to retrace their steps, and to choose the proper path toward complete understanding. Thus Lashley was able to demonstrate many of the themes which were central to this seminal essay on speech production. First, he showed how **slips of the tongue** (or the computer keyboard) provide vivid insights into our understanding of how speech is formulated. Second, he illustrated the power of **priming** in guiding the direction of speech production and comprehension. Because Lashley first talked about 'writing', his audience was primed to hear the phrase again, and this is what confused them initially when they heard 'rapid righting' as part of an utterance about a canoe. Note also that it is possible that priming works in the production process as well.

A critical insight from this example, and from Lashley's essay as a whole, is the way it demonstrates how both the production and the comprehension of speech is largely a linear process. The audience didn't know that Lashley had purposely misled their comprehension until they suddenly heard something about 'saving the contents of the capsized canoe'. People tend to produce and comprehend sentences in a linear way, and for comprehension, each additional piece of information we receive has the potential to force us to revamp our understanding of what we have already heard. The comprehension of the 'canoe' example, taken from Lashley's lecture and subsequently published paper, lends credence to the notion that, in several ways, production and comprehension are similar. Both are largely sequential, both are affected by priming, and they both depend, to a large degree, on the constant winnowing of implausible alternatives at each juncture in our stream of speech.

Slips of the tongue

Think back to the example at the beginning of this chapter of how we tend to ignore the complexity of strolling down a flight of stairs until we trip. Over the past few decades, psycholinguists have become excited about a new way of discovering how we put words into our mouths: they look at what happens when we trip over our tongues. Unlike stammering or aphasia (linguistic loss due to brain damage), slips of the tongue, or typographical mistakes, are normal, everyday occurrences which pervade our speaking and our writing. And because of this, as soon as our friends spot our mistake, or we happen to catch the goof ourselves, we can immediately backtrack and correct. However, when speech and language disintegrate into clear pathologies, as they do in stammering and aphasia (to be discussed in Chapter 5), there appears to be no recourse, and the error remains uncorrectable and uncorrected. So we can see why slips of the tongue provide the data that delight psycholinguists; they allow us to peek in on the production process because we know what the speaker intended to say, but the unintentional mistake freezes the production process momentarily and catches the linguistic mechanism in one instance of production.

The use of linguistic deviations as data for scientific investigation is a new phenomenon, but the recognition of speech errors goes back more than a century. **Spoonerisms**, like the unfortunate use of 'the breast in bed' instead of 'the best in bread', are named after the Victorian cleric and teacher, William Spooner, who reputedly blundered through many a lecture or sermon with infamous slips in speech production. He called a group of Welsh miners 'you noble tons of soil' and supposedly scolded an errant student by saying, 'you have hissed all my mystery lectures; in fact, you have tasted the whole worm!' Spoonerisms then are slips of the tongue in which an actual word or phrase is created, often with a humorous twist to the meaning which was intended.

The mention of verbal miscues, especially ones like the 'bread' example just cited, evokes a discussion of Freudian slips. In one of his earliest treatises, *Psychopathology of Everyday Life*, Sigmund Freud hypothesized that slips of the tongue were important because, like dreams, they help to reveal the unconscious mind. But most psycholinguists have ignored Freudian interpretations of speech errors for a variety of reasons. For one thing, although slips like 'the breast in bed' appear to be embarrassingly indicative of an unconscious desire, a coldly empirical approach to this mistake would propose at least two explanations for the source of this illicit feeling: either the speaker was sexually provoked (and was unconsciously thinking about the first noun in the phrase), or he was actually fixating on the second noun because he was so exhausted! Here, we run into exactly the same problem we faced earlier when we tried to define what the conceptualization stage for speech consisted of; we are in danger of becoming too **mentalistic**—that is, relying on logic and intuition rather than experimental evidence—in our attempts to fathom what exactly puts words into people's mouths. A more important reason why psycholinguists tend to ignore Freudian analyses of why who said what is because, irrespective of their meaning, the formulation of slips of the tongue reveals important linguistic patterns—patterns that also pervade normal and natural speech. That is, what is relevant to psycholinguistics is not *what* is being said, but *how* it is being said, or, to be precise, misspoken.

But before leaving Freud, it might be illuminating to examine some recent work in the psychology of language that attempts to wed the Freudian, mentalistic tradition of psychology with the experimental school which so strongly colors contemporary psycholinguistics. This was the goal of an experiment in which university students were asked to read aloud two, unrelated words flashed quickly in front of them on a computer screen. For example, the subjects might have seen 'barn door' instantaneously flashed in front of them, and they either read them correctly, or, as was often the case, because of the pressure of time, came up with a slip of the tongue, such as 'darn bore'. There were three different situations: a control—or normal—situation, where the subjects had no distractions; a second situation where subjects knew that they might receive a small electrical shock at any moment, and a third situation, where they performed the task in a state of slight sexual arousal (the subjects were all male, and the experimenter was an attractive and well-dressed female). Here are examples of two stimuli phrases which were flashed to all three groups.

(1) sham dock   (2) past fashion

Although most of the subjects were accurate most of the time under all three conditions, the slips of the tongue which did occur differed significantly among the three groups. The control group tended to make arbitrary errors, such as 'darn bore', but the two experimental conditions tended to elicit two different kinds of slips. When (1) was flashed to the subjects who were in the group that was threatened with a potential electrical discharge, they, much more frequently than the other two groups, came up with the slip 'damn shock'. And when (2) was shown to the group with the attractive female experimenter, they, as you have already anticipated, came up with the phrase 'fast passion' much more frequently than the others. This experiment comes about as close as we can expect to get to testing Freud's ideas under laboratory conditions, or to catching a glimpse of the conceptualization stage of speech production. Be that as it may, our focus here is on formulation, and from all of the examples cited so far, we can readily see that slips of the tongue are not a random, haphazard zigzagging of the production mechanism, like quarks in a cloud chamber. Sounds and words are not thrown together arbitrarily; there is a clear, linear and hierarchical order to the way in which we put words into our mouths.

There has been a long and rich tradition of examining speech errors in psycholinguistics as a window to the formulation process and not as a reflection of some Freudian motivation. Based on examples gleaned over the years, researchers have been able to demonstrate that these superficially trivial quirks of communication are quite useful in offering insights about how speech is formulated. For one thing, there is sure evidence from this data that the units of speech, such as 'phoneme' and 'morpheme', which linguists have proposed and discussed for many years are **psychologically real**. This means that when we mis-speak, we make errors within the boundaries and the framework of a certain language structure, as if we had intentionally planned our slips to fit an appropriate linguistic slot. Mistakes do not pop out just anywhere when we speak, they occur at predictable points and follow predictable patterns. It is almost as if we think about syllables, words, and phrases as we are formulating what we are going to say, and this is why psycholinguists find slips of the tongue insightful. Let us review some of this evidence.

Linguists divide sounds into vowels and consonants and sub-categorize each of these into various phonetic groupings. Speech errors seem to follow the phonetic classifications established by linguists and rarely, if ever, cross over these linguistic boundaries. Consider the following examples.

(1) a reading list   a *l*eading list
(2) big and fat   *p*ig and fat
(3) fill the pool   f*oo*l the p*i*ll
(4) drop a bomb   *b*op a *dr*omb

As trivial and silly as these mistakes may appear initially, they actually tell us a great deal about the organization of the English language. The anticipation of [l] in the third word in (1), creates the substitution of [l] for [r] in the second word. Phoneticians point out that [l] and [r] are two consonants which share many phonetic features for example, both are pronounced in the same part of the mouth, so that this type of substitution would always be likely. There is no such phonetic explanation for a substitution of [l] for [sh] (e.g. '*sh*opping list' becoming '*l*opping list'), and, in fact, whereas flip-flops of [l] and [r] for each other pervade the miscue data, transpositions of [l] or [r] for sounds like [sh] are exceedingly rare. The second example is a bit more subtle, because at first sight it seems that [p] is randomly introduced into the phrase from nowhere. But again, linguistic analysis gives a clear explanation. The phonetic feature of voicelessness of the following [f] in fat seems to be anticipated when the speaker is about to produce the [b] in the first word of phrase (2). As it turns out, the voiceless equivalent of the consonant [b] is [p]. Although we are focusing on sound structure in these first few examples, it is also possible that speakers are simultaneously being influenced by other linguistic factors, so that the person who misspoke 'pig and fat' may have also been gently nudged by the semantic association between these words.

In (3) we see the psychological reality of the contrast between vowels and consonants in the minds of speakers. The vowels in the two words replace each other. It is theoretically possible for vowels to substitute for consonants and vice versa, but again, this rarely occurs because they are so distinct linguistically. Finally, in (4) we see how speech errors follow rules about what consonants can go together to form clusters. We can't just put any two consonants together in English, or in any other language for that matter: although we have [dr] in 'drop' and [st] in 'stick', we have no words that begin with [sr] like 'srop' or even worse, [dt] as in 'dtick'. So even though there is no word 'drom' in English, the [dr] cluster that the slip in (4) creates is permissible, and it tells linguists that people who come up with odd expressions like these still follow the sound patterns of English.

Slips of the tongue also reveal that when we formulate speech, we are not only influenced by the sound system of the language we are speaking, we are also conditioned by the way words are put together in that language. Consider the following examples as evidence of the psychological reality of **morphology**—the way words are organized and structured in a language.

(5) sesame seed crackers	sesame *street* crackers
(6) rules of word formation	*words* of *rule* formation
(7) a New Yorker	a New *Yorkan*
(8) the derivation of	the *derival* of

Unlike the first set of examples, these slips do not involve individual sounds; rather, they seem to reflect a higher level of linguistic organization because they are associated with complete words, or with significant parts of words. (5) and (6) are very common examples, and they remind us of the spoonerisms discussed earlier. Notice how the misspoken forms still adhere to normal patterns of word usage. For example 'Sesame Street crackers' might be a brand of cracker named after the children's TV show. Note too the manner in which (6) adheres to a regular word pattern in English. A 'four-door sedan' has four doors, an 'apple pie' is made of apples. A common error by learners of English is to call these objects a 'four-doors sedan' and 'apples pie', following the logical, but non-English pattern of extending the plural to the formation of noun phrases. But native speakers, who follow the rules of word formation, do not simply swap the two words that are reversed in (6) and say 'word of rules formation'. Even during the micromomentary process of formulating their speech, they follow the regular and established pattern.

Examples (7) and (8) are further elaborations of this same theme, but in this case, the suffix slots are exchanged while the original words remain the same. The person who misspoke (7) might have been thinking, if an 'American' is someone who lives in America, why isn't a resident of New York a 'New Yorkan?' And by the same logic, if 'arrival' is the noun form of the verb 'arrive', why isn't the noun form of 'to derive', 'derival?' Once again we witness the way slips of the tongue provide psycholinguistic insights into the production of speech; they help us see how speakers arrive at derivations.

Speech errors are also helpful in revealing a third level of language processing at the formulation stage; they give support to the notion that utterances are not just strings of sounds and linear sequences of words, but are formed into larger structural units.

This is demonstrated in examples (9) and (10).

(9) he swam in the pool   he *swimmed* in the pool
(10) the children are in the park   the *childs* are in the park

These mistakes are much less common than the swapping of words and parts of words that we find in spoonerisms and similar constructions, but their occurrence, however rare, tells us something about the way grammar affects the formulation process. Those familiar with the speech and writing of non-native users of English will recognize these goofs as learner errors, but the big difference between learner errors and the slips exemplified by (9) and (10) is that native speakers almost always correct themselves when they err; learners of English, on the other hand, experience great difficulty recognizing exactly what was wrong and how to rectify it. Almost immediately after saying (10), for example, a native speaker might stop and say 'I mean *children*'. Learners, upon recognizing that they said something wrong in a sentence like (10), or, more commonly, having it pointed out to them, will often miscorrect the original error and come out with something like 'I mean *childrens*'. The fact that native speakers correct themselves shows that they are also paying attention to grammar, in addition to concentrating at the sound and word levels of the language. It is no accident that these last examples all involve irregular words. It looks very much as if the speaker has chosen the words and the slots which they fill, and at the last moment, forgotten to choose the right verb or noun form. The errors suggest that speakers organize their utterances into smaller groups of words, like noun phrases, or clauses with a main verb, and having filled these groups with the appropriate lexical items which express the intended meaning, the speakers finally add the appropriate grammatical inflections. Almost always, this complicated process is completed fluently and accurately, and only occasionally, as in these examples, does the formulation of speech slip up. But when it does, it provides us with a glimpse of the production process.

The planning of higher levels of speech

Another way of trying to understand the process of producing language is to analyze the steps we have to take and the decisions we have to make in order to produce an intended utterance.

Suppose, for example, that you might want to give a response, either spoken or written, in a certain situation. Let's say you are in a discussion with a friend about the importance of a particular matter, and your friend asks for your opinion about the gravity of the situation. You decide to frame a response, and for whatever reason, you choose to conceptualize the idea that the matter was not important. How do you go ahead and formulate this concept linguistically? Granted, you are constrained by all the phonological, lexical, and grammatical patterns of English which were exemplified and supported by the slip of the tongue data just discussed, but, despite all these rules and patterns, there is still a great deal of flexibility in what you say and how you say it.

Of course, how we choose to formulate what we are about to say or write is influenced by such factors as politeness or social appropriateness. These extremely important variables are not usually dealt with in the relatively asocial circles of psycholinguistics, but they are central to the concerns of linguists who investigate **pragmatics**—the study of what people mean when they use language in normal social interaction, or those who study **sociolinguistics**—the study of why we say what to whom, when, and where. But just within the narrow confines of how we formulate a simple concept such as 'not important' into actual words, following the rules of the language we have chosen to speak, and disregarding all the complicated nuances of pragmatics and sociolinguistics, we still have many choices to consider. Given all the decisions we are forced to make every time we begin to open our mouth, it is quite astonishing that conversations aren't painfully slow trickles of syllables, dripping intermittently from tongue-tied interlocutors. In fact, they are often the reverse—cascading torrents of speech pouring so rapidly and so easily that conversants overlap and interrupt each other in their eagerness to fill the silence.

We will freeze this fictional conversation at the very instant when one speaker decides to put the concept 'not important' into words. Many choices come to mind. Should the concept be expressed lexically, that is through the choice of a word, or should it be expressed by means of a syntactic pattern? Supposing the speaker makes the first choice, further alternatives still remain. Will the word chosen be grammatically negative, as in (a), or affirmative? If the latter, will the word be an antonym, or opposite of 'important' as in (b), or will it contain an explicit negative prefix like *un-* in (c)?

(a) It's *nothing*.
(b) It's *trivial*.
(c) It's *unimportant*.

It may seem a bit peculiar to differentiate among these three choices by calling the first negative and the other two affirmative, because they all convey the same idea, that the speaker believes the situation is *not* important. But language is not always as it seems, a fact that most native speakers are blithely unaware of and one that allows psycholinguists to make a living. Think, for a moment, about one very common way of asking questions in English—by placing a tag at the end of an utterance. You've probably asked questions like this a lot, haven't you? Observe that an affirmative sentence, like the tag question immediately preceding this one, uses a negative tag, and vice versa, so if we choose to formulate a negative sentence, then the tag is affirmative. You're not confused about this, are you? Let us go back to our three examples and see what happens when we transform these sentences into tag questions.

(d) It's nothing, *is* it?
(e) It's trivial, *isn't* it?
(f) It's unimportant, *isn't* it?

The affirmative tag '**is** it' in (d) tells us that even though there is no overt negation in this short response, it is still considered grammatically negative. If it weren't, it would have a negative tag at the end, wouldn't it? In contrast, both (e) and (f) must have negative tags because they are both grammatically affirmative phrases. Nevertheless, they are not similar: (e) expresses the concept of 'not important' by choosing an antonym; (f) says the same thing by using a negative prefix with 'important'. And the choice of prefix in (f) is an additional complication, because English proffers a wide range of potential prefixes. Some words take several choices (for example *un*European, *non*-European, *anti*-European), but even words like 'important', which only take *un*-, create a production problem. When speakers choose 'trivial', the only thing they have to remember is the word itself, but when they select a word which takes a negative prefix, they have to recall which one to use. Again, we often fail to realize the complexity of the production process until we see it fall apart, as in the *in*correct choice of a prefix by a learner (for example *un*possible and *dis*important).

Let us go back now to the initial choice the speaker made. Recall that the first alternative the speaker had in formulating the concept 'not important', was whether to express the negative response lexically—via words, or grammatically—via the use of syntactic negation. Let us suppose the second alternative was picked, creating the series of choices exemplified by sentences (g) and (h).

(g) It *isn't* important.
(h) It's *not* important.

You may have to glance at these twice to catch the slight differences between them, and they are so minimal that you might be provoked into using some of the earlier examples: the differences are nothing; they're trivial! But if the speaker has chosen to express the negation grammatically rather than through word choice, important differences can be indicated by means of stress. Normally, the contracted negative in (g) is chosen because negation is typically not the focus of our attention, but (h) offers an effective way of emphasizing negation. Supposing you are in an argumentative state, and your conversational partner keeps insisting that the situation is desperate; (h) allows you to be emphatic about your denial. Put tersely, the difference between the two sentences is that in (g) the negative is not usually stressed, but in (h) it receives unusual stress.

The significance of these slight differences may seem minimal within the context of the myriad sounds, words, and sentences that comprise our daily staple of communication, but along with the slip of the tongue examples, they demonstrate the enormous number and intricacy of choices facing a speaker, or a writer, at this important stage of formulation.

Articulation

We have spent considerable time examining the second stage of speech production, and for good reason. Like the operation of a computer program during word processing, the formulation stage of speech involves thousands of split-second decisions regarding the hierarchical and sequential selection of myriads of potential segments. But this third stage of articulation is similar to what happens when all of those bits of information selected by a word processing program go from your computer to your printer; unless this vast amount of electrical data is 'articulated' into letters of the alphabet and successfully printed, no message is received. In fact, if the printer is not functioning properly, there is no evidence that the message was ever even composed. So, too, with the production of speech. Unless all of the electrical impulses streaming from your brain in the form of speech are transformed into audible and comprehensible articulations, no words are heard and nothing is communicated. The conceptualization stage might pompously perceive itself as the primary and ultimate composer of communication, and the formulation stage might pride itself as the conductor and orchestrator of speech sounds, but without the instruments of articulation, the music of our voices remains unheard and unappreciated. Like the operations of a printer or the playing of instruments then, the articulation of speech sounds is a vital third stage of production and, quite naturally, attracts the interest of psycholinguists.

As recently as the 1960s, linguists upheld the common sensical and seemingly incontrovertible notion that the chest, throat, and mouth were anatomical organs designed solely for biological functions. Only in a secondary way could they be considered the organs of speech. Surely, the basic function of our lungs is to exchange oxygen for carbon dioxide, not to produce syllables and, most assuredly, the primary use of our teeth is for chewing, not for the articulation of sounds like [t] and [d]? True as these assertions may be, they do not preclude the possibility that some organs may have been shaped in their recent evolutionary history to enhance the production of human speech sounds. Some thirty years ago Eric Lenneberg, a psycholinguist, showed that whereas the majority of these organs have primarily evolved to serve essential biological functions such as respiration and ingestion, a few of them have adopted secondary functions connected with the enhancement of speech articulation. In a few cases, there are organs that have changed anatomically to fit this new role as speech articulator. So dramatic are the changes that they differ physically from the corresponding organs in closely related species like chimpanzees.

Perhaps the most dramatic example of an organ which has adapted itself for human articulation is the larynx—the 'voice box' which houses our vocal cords. Like all the other speech organs, the larynx did not initially evolve with the specific function of helping humans to articulate language. For one thing, the vocal cords in all animals possessing a larynx serve as a kind of emergency trap door which can prevent foreign matter, such as bits of food, from falling from the mouth down the pharyngeal tube and through the trachea into the lungs. When bits of debris do manage to find their way down these passageways, the vocal cords help control explosions of air from the lungs to cough this potentially life-threatening jetsam back up out of the mouth. The larynx thus helps keep the respiratory tract clear, but it serves another primary function which is just the opposite of coughing. By squeezing tightly closed, it can trap air in the chest cavity and create a solid fulcrum for the limbs to work against when heavy physical exertion is required. However, in the case of our species we could claim that speech has now become the primary function of the larynx and the other, original purposes of the voice box have diminished to secondary stature.

Evidence for the evolutionary modification of the human larynx to create speech is quite dramatic. Lenneberg and others have documented several speech-enhancing characteristics of the voice box that are unique to humans and are absent in other mammals, even the primates like chimps and gorillas. No wonder then that they have remained unable to master articulate speech. The most striking difference between humans and all other animals in this area of the body is the position of the larynx. In all other animals, the larynx is found high in the throat, crammed behind the tongue, an exceedingly advantageous position for preventing debris from entering the trachea, for it can be trapped immediately as it leaves the mouth. But this is not true for us. Feel your neck and find your larynx (or 'Adam's apple'). You will locate about halfway down, almost touching the top of a high-collared shirt or blouse. Consider the awful consequences of this anatomical deviation from natural evolution. Unlike all other animals, our emergency trap door cannot stop foreign matter as soon as it leaves the mouth. It is so far down that a passageway, called the pharynx, has been created into which debris can easily fall, and we, among all creatures, are the most susceptible to choking. Why does nature deviate in this destructive manner for humans?

The advantages of the lower voice box reside in the way this arrangement serves to embellish the articulation of speech sounds. Unlike other mammals whose highly-positioned larynx virtually precludes the existence of a pharyngeal tube linking the back of the mouth with the opening of the vocal cords, the pharynx benefits the production of speech in at least two ways. It creates a new source of speech sounds—the 'throaty' consonants of Arabic, or the initial consonant of the two words in the English salutation, 'Hi Harry!' A pharyngeal tube also increases **resonance** by adding extra acoustic space to the already existing oral and nasal cavities. The addition of a pharynx to the vocal repertoire is not unlike the addition of a cello to the duet of a violin and viola; the timbre of the human voice is that much richer, thanks to the added instrument. Another enormous benefit of the lowered larynx is the way it frees up the back of the tongue so that the tongue root can maneuver and create more speech sounds. The contrast between the vowels in the words 'look' and 'Luke' is made largely by subtle movements of the tongue root, movements that no other animals are capable of performing. So the linguistic advantages outweigh the physiological disadvantages, and if the emergence of language is as vital to our evolutionary history as most anthropologists believe, and if language is so indispensable to our species, it is no exaggeration to claim that the descent of the larynx has permitted the ascent of mankind!

Given the anatomy of articulation we have been endowed with, what do we know about the programming of articulation? How do sounds trip so miraculously off the tips of our tongues once speech is conceptualized and formulated? It is easy to assume that speech sounds are produced in a linear, sequential fashion, like cars off an assembly line, but a closer analogy might be to the team effort that goes into producing a batch of cookies. While one person might be chopping the walnuts, another might be preparing the cookie dough, while a third might be preheating the oven and greasing the cookie sheets. So too in the production of speech sounds. The process might appear to be linear, but the lungs, larynx, and lips may be working all at the same time, and **coarticulation** is the norm, not the exception. That is, in the production of any single sound, a lot of anatomical effort is devoted to performing several different movements simultaneously.

Consider just one sound, the second [k] (spelled, of course, with a 'qu') in the expression: 'Keep *qu*iet kid!' Let us begin by contrasting the second [k] with the first (in 'keep') and the last (in 'kid'). All three of these sounds are *dorsovelar* which means they are made in the back of the mouth. The back of the tongue (the *dorsum*) hunches up and touches the soft palate at the back of the mouth (the *velum*) to stop the flow of air momentarily to produce the consonant [k]. But the process is much more complicated than this, because every sound in the stream of speech is affected by the sounds which swim around it. None of the [k]s in this particular phrase is preceded by any sound which would demonstrably affect its pronunciation but each is followed by sounds which do affect articulation. The first and last are followed by a vowel pronounced in the front of the mouth, so the [k] in 'keep' and the [k] in 'kid' slide forward a bit from their usual position in the back. It is almost as if the tongue were at the starting line of a sprint and was trying to inch up a bit to get a head start in the race to those front vowels. There is a double contrast between the [k] in 'quiet' and the first and the last [k]'s. First, because the vowel in this word at least begins with a sound in the back of the mouth (the initial [a] of the diphthong [ai]), the [k] in this word does not inch forward at all, but actually sits well back in order to hit the following back vowel. Secondly, because 'qu' is actually a cluster [kw] and not a single sound, the initial [k] is rounded in anticipation of the following [w]. In other words, the lips assume an 'o' position when we begin to articulate 'quiet', whereas they remained flat and unrounded in the production of the first and last words. Try reproducing this phrase in front of the mirror, and you'll obtain visual evidence of the effects of coarticulation; the mouth momentarily puckers up when you begin to pronounce 'quiet'. Here we observe the complexity of articulation. Sounds do not emerge as segments strung together sequentially; they are mixed and melded, with each sound shaping its neighbors while concurrently being shaped themselves.

Psycholinguists have developed a number of competing models to try to account for the complexity of speech articulation, and they have tried to employ various sources of evidence to peek into this complicated process, but much of articulation remains a mystery. For example, despite the increasing sophistication of modern neurology and the development of techniques such as **Positron Emission Tomography** (**PET**) scans to examine the way the human brain programs neuromuscular movements, we still have little understanding of how the cerebral software programs the anatomical printer to articulate sounds in such a glib manner. Let us narrow the issue down to one simple question. How does the tongue 'know' to cheat a little bit ahead in the first and last words of the phrase described in the paragraph above, but 'know' not to inch forward in the second word. And how do the lips 'know' when to pucker up? It would be impossibly difficult to explain the rapidity and accuracy of articulation in such closely related phrases simply as a chain of habits acquired in a linear way.

We see then that even at this seemingly uncreative and mechanical aspect of speech production, complexity and mystery abound, and speaking ceases to appear a simple and mundane act. Speech production does not end with articulation, however; the fourth and final stage of production is the process of self-monitoring.

Self-monitoring

Earlier, during our review of slips of the tongue, it was noted that the production process sometimes goes awry and speakers will verbally misstep, especially with irregular or more unusual forms. Almost always, however, they instantly catch themselves, retreat a step, and correctly recreate the intended sequence, as in (1) and (2).

(1) The last I *knowed* about it {I mean *knew* about it}, he had left Vancouver.

(2) She was so *drank* {I mean *drunk*}, that we decided to drive her home.

In contrast to the conceptualization and formulation stages of production but similar to the articulation stage which we just reviewed, it seems that at this final stage of self-monitoring we have direct evidence of what is happening when people compose speech. Interlocutors not only produce speech and listen to one another when conversing, they also seem to keep one ear open on what they themselves are saying, and if they catch something amiss, they are quick to amend the goof and then continue to converse.

All speakers and writers of any language, regardless of their degree of native fluency, commit linguistic blunders. To err is human. Common to all speakers too is the way in which fluency seems inversely proportional to the amount of attention they pay to the production process. It also appears to vary inversely in proportion to the degree of stress they are under, or the quantity of certain beverages they have imbibed! S. Pit Corder, a pioneer in the field of **Second Language Acquisition (SLA)** classified these slips of the tongue and the pen as **mistakes**. The examples listed earlier in this chapter, or goofs like the typos and misspellings we are all responsible for from time to time, are mistakes, whether they come from native or non-native mouths and fingers. Mistakes are production problems; they are the troubles you have with your linguistic printer, not with the original software. The true test of a mistake is to see whether or not it is corrected, and (1) and (2) above, as well as most of the other illustrations we have covered, are surely mistakes under this definition. **Errors**, on the other hand, are committed only by non-native speakers (NNSs) according to Corder. Even when the speech gaffe is pointed out to NNSs, they have difficulty correcting it. For example when NNSs goof up in the production of irregular verbs, as beginning learners of English often do, they frequently fail to notice that they erred in what they said or wrote. Even when they are told that they erred, unlike the native speakers exemplified in (1) and (2), NNSs do not immediately replace the deviancy with the correct form.

The fact that native speakers do not commit 'errors' (in Corder's sense of the word) coupled with the fact that they often produce 'mistakes' which they almost immediately self-correct, reveals three insights into the production process. First and most transparently, it demonstrates that speakers (and writers) are constantly self-editing. Production is not a one-way transmission of messages; it is a self-regulating process with a **feedback loop** to ensure that each previous stage of output was accurate. Second, it suggests that speakers are intuitively sensitive to what stage of the production process went awry, if indeed a mistake was made. Speakers and writers are quickly capable of readjusting a message at the stages of conceptualization, formulation, or articulation, depending on where they noticed the breakdown in production occurred. Finally, the fact that native speakers can monitor and quickly correct any mistakes in linguistic output proves Chomsky's contention that there is a distinction between **performance** and **competence**. The former refers to the words we say or write, the overt manifestation of our ability in a language; the latter describes our tacit, intuitive knowledge about the language or languages we have mastered. At this final level of production, competence monitors performance to ensure that our production is accurate.

There are several different ways native speakers edit their linguistic performance. Psycholinguists have studied the kinds of self-repairs speakers make and have discovered some significant contrasts in the ways they monitor their output. When speakers were dissatisfied with the social or situational appropriateness of their speech (i.e. their choices were wrong at the very beginning, at the conceptualization stage), they were much more likely to backtrack and begin the utterance all over again; however, if speakers were content with the conceptualization of their utterance, but had somehow goofed up at the formulation or articulation stages, they were less likely to start afresh. They would retreat a few syllables or words to the linguistic juncture in the utterance where plans began to fall apart, and renew the sentence from that point, as seen back in examples (1) and (2).

Once more we witness the way in which language and speech provide windows to human cognitive processing. Evidence appears strong that stage models of production, such as those posited by Levelt and described in this chapter, accurately reflect the manner in which people produce and edit conversations or compositions.

Along with mistakes, such as slips of the tongue, psycholinguists have also relied on the trivial and sometimes annoying hesitations which punctuate our unplanned, spoken discourse to gain insights into the ways in which we monitor the language we produce.

(3) I think it costs just about ... *uh* ... twenty-five dollars.
(4) They have to try to ... *uh* ... contact an attorney.

Hesitations like those exemplified in (3) and (4), or the ubiquitous 'y'know' which pervades a great deal of contemporary conversation, are not mistakes—certainly not in the sense that the term has been defined and illustrated here. Nevertheless, they do seem to indicate a lack of fluency. But however clumsy they might appear to an articulate speaker of the language, they are not random, but rule-governed, and hence they are of interest to psycholinguists. Notice how the hesitations in (3) and (4) appear at a crucial point in the sentence—before the object of the verb in (3) and before the complement of the verb in (4). The intrusive 'uh' suggest that the conceptualization phase is still in the process of selecting the information to appear at the end of the sentence, after the verb in these examples, and so the speaker pauses in mid-utterance to allow the computer to program the last part of the message to be printed. However awkward these hesitations might sound, they reflect the grammatical structure of the language being spoken, and they would almost never violate linguistic constraints. We very rarely find utterances like (5) and (6).

(5) I think it costs just ... *uh* ... about twenty-five dollars.
(6) They have ... *uh* ... to try to contact an attorney.

'Just about' and 'have to' function as linguistic units, so it is improbable that the speaker would hesitate in the middle of either one, after having already chosen to fill the linguistic slot of the utterance with those phrases.

One final point about self-monitoring. It contrasts markedly with the dated and very inaccurate depiction of communication as consisting of a message that speaker A sends to listener B. The attested presence of a self-monitoring stage presumes that people don't just communicate with others, they communicate with themselves; they don't just listen to others, they listen to themselves. Communication is not a one-way broadcast of a signal, but it is an interactive process, involving not just the interaction *between* the interlocutors but also the interaction *within* each individual speaker. The self-editing process confirms for psycholinguistics what has long been known to exist in most biological functions of the body—the presence of feedback loops. Speech production (or written composition) is not a linear 'one-way' process; it is a parallel, 'two-way' system involving both output and the concurrent editing and modulation of that output.

Let us go back to the theme with which we began this chapter. All of the complexities of production which we have reviewed here are largely overlooked by speakers. Language generally flows effortlessly, and even our hesitations, slips, and backtrackings are so swiftly executed that they go mostly unnoticed. It is only when this marvelously evolved and efficient instrument of communication breaks down that we appreciate its intricacy. And it is also only then that we begin to glean significant psycholinguistic insights.

4
Comprehension: understanding what we hear and read

Understanding language, like producing it, is such an automatic task that it may appear to be a relatively straightforward process. Sounds or letters strike our ears or eyes in a swift and linear fashion creating words, which in turn very quickly form phrases, clauses, and sentences so that comprehension seems to be nothing more than the recognition of a sequential string of linguistic symbols, albeit at a very rapid pace. What appears on the surface to be linguistically transparent, however, turns out to be almost impenetrably complex from the perspective of psycholinguistics. What is apparent from the vast research into the comprehension of spoken and written language is that people do not process linguistic information in a neat, linear fashion; they do not move smoothly from one linguistic level to another as if they were riding a lift that began on the ground floor of phonology and finally stopped at the top floor of meaning. The research shows that in most situations, listeners and readers use a great deal of information other than the actual language being produced to help them decipher the linguistic symbols they hear or see.

The comprehension of sounds

Here is a simple example of how what we hear is influenced by psycholinguistic variables and is not just the accurate perception of the sequences of sounds or words that hit our ears. In one psycholinguistic experiment, a set of sentences was played to a group of listeners who were asked to write down the sixth word in each of the following sentences.

(1) It was found that the _eel was on the axle.
(2) It was found that the _eel was on the shoe.
(3) It was found that the _eel was on the orange.
(4) It was found that the _eel was on the table.

Notice that in every case, the subjects heard *eel* as the key word in the sentence, but most of the subjects claimed they had heard a different word for each example- specifically, *wheel* for (1), *heel* for (2), *peel* for (3), and *meal* for (4). The insertion of a different missing sound (phoneme) to create a separate but appropriate '*eel*' word in each sentence is called the **phoneme restoration effect**. Under these conditions, listeners do not accurately record what they hear; rather, they report what they expected to hear from the context, even if it means they must add a sound that was never actually spoken at the beginning of the target word. Several simple but significant observations can be drawn from this sample of the early psycholinguistic research into the nature of comprehension.

First of all, as just illustrated, people don't necessarily hear each of the words spoken to them. Comprehension is not the passive recording of whatever is heard or seen; listeners are not tape recorders nor readers video cameras. Second, comprehension is strongly influenced by even the slightest of changes in discourse which the listener is attending to. In these examples, except for the last word, each of these sentences is identical. Finally, comprehension is not a simple item-by-item analysis of words in a linear sequence. We don't read or hear the same way we count digits sequentially from one to ten. Listeners and readers process chunks of information and sometimes wait to make decisions on what is comprehended until much later in the sequence. It is the last—not the sixth or 'target'—word in each of the four examples above which dictated what the listeners in the experiment reported they heard. We don't seem to listen to each word individually and comprehend its meaning in isolation; we seek contextual consistency and plausibility, even if it comes to adding a sound or inventing a word that wasn't actually spoken. This chapter then reviews some of the ways in which psycholinguistic processes affect the way listeners and readers comprehend language.

Although, in the course of everyday conversation, we don't hear vowels and consonants as isolated sounds, we can, with the help of machines, measure acoustic information extremely precisely. The /p/ in the following English words is pronounced slightly differently depending on where it occurs in the word or what other sounds follow it. The initial /p/ of 'pool' is pronounced with puckered lips but the 'same' /p/ in 'peel' is spoken with the lips spread, and neither of these /p/'s sound quite like the /p/ in 'spring'. Although these details may seem trivial to a native speaker of English, they are significant enough acoustically to be heard as contrasting phonemes in other languages. Despite these differences, and other variations of /p/ that could be cited in countless other examples, native speakers of English claim they hear and pronounce the same /p/ sound. Notice that for these and most of the other examples, we spell the sound with the letter 'p' and furthermore, despite all the variations in /p/, native speakers of English almost never confuse any manifestation of the /p/ sound with /b/, which is acoustically very similar. Recall that in the discussion of the articulation stage in Chapter 3, we saw that there was a sizeable phonetic difference between the initial /k/s of 'keep' and 'kid' and the /k/ sound which begins the word 'cool'. Phoneticians have been fairly successful in writing rules that predict which precise acoustic form of /p/ is pronounced (or heard) under which phonetic condition; nevertheless, they have been unable to explain how this variation is processed by the mind or how all the phonetic differences which occur among all the many languages of the world can be accounted for in terms of the common, universal processes of perception that are shared by all humans. Although the exact details of this acoustic processing have yet to be resolved, psycholinguists have come up with some explanations for this most fundamental level of comprehension.

Suppose we are engaged in conversation with a friend and are discussing two other acquaintances with similar sounding names—'Benny' and 'Penny'. What phonetic information do we employ as we listen to distinguish these names which are identical in pronunciation except for the initial consonant? Phoneticians have discovered that the main feature which English speakers attend to, albeit unconsciously, is the **Voice Onset Timing** (**VOT**) of the initial consonant. Using instruments which are sensitive enough to measure contrasts as small as milliseconds in the duration of speech sounds, they have demonstrated that the most significant acoustic different between English consonants like /b/ and /p/ is the length of time it takes between the initial puff of air that begins these sounds, and the onset of voicing in the throat that initiates any vowel sound which follows the consonants. Since almost all the other phonetic features of this consonantal pair are identical, the crucial clue that separates the voiced /b/ and its voiceless counterpart /p/ is a VOT of a scant 50 milliseconds. This means that the correct comprehension of the name 'Penny', as opposed to the mistaken recognition of the similar sounding 'Benny', depends on an ability to perceive a voicing delay of one-twentieth of a second! The simple task of recognizing which person is being referred to during a conversation is based on your ability to isolate one subtle phonological feature from the myriad sounds hitting your ear and to make a split-second judgment. How do speakers of English, or any language for that matter, make these incredibly difficult decisions about speech so rapidly and so accurately?

It appears that the acquisition of this phonetic ability cannot be completely explained only by exposure to, or instruction in, the language. In other words, native speakers do not acquire all of this acoustic information from direct experience with language, and as we learned in Chapter 2, parents and caretakers do not provide explicit instruction on these matters. Even phoneticians do not subject their children to hours of nursery training listening to minimal pairs like 'pie' versus 'buy'. Psycholinguists have discovered through careful experimentation that humans are actually born with the ability to focus in on VOT differences in the speech sounds they hear, and they have proven that rather than perceiving VOT contrasts as a continuum, people tend to categorize these minute phonetic differences in a non-continual, binary fashion.

All of this has been decisively documented in experiments where native speakers of English listened to artificially created consonant sounds with gradually lengthening VOTs and were asked to judge whether the syllables they heard began with a voiced consonant (like /b/ which has a short VOT) and a voiceless one (like /p/ which, as was just pointed out, has a VOT lag of about 50 milliseconds). When subjects heard sounds with a VOT of about 25 milliseconds, about halfway between a /b/ and a /p/, they rarely judged the sound to be 50% voiceless and 50% voiced, they classified it as one sound or the other. This phenomenon is called **categorical perception**. Psycholinguists have been able to prove the presence of categorical perception in very young infants, through a series of cleverly designed experiments. And in equally ingenious research with several species of animals, they have found, by and large, that this kind of all-or-nothing acoustic perception does not exist in other species. Categorical perception is seemingly unique to human beings, and appears to qualify as one aspect of universal grammar (UG), the genetic propensity for comprehending and producing language which most psycholinguists believe is a uniquely human endowment. These experiments with VOT perception in human infants are one of the few solid pieces of evidence we have that UG exists and that at least part of human language is **modular**—that is, some parts of language reside in the mind or brain as an independent system or module.

Although categorical perception of VOT is an ability children are born with, it is also influenced by the linguistic environment a child is raised in. Here lies the second part of the puzzle of how native speakers of English grow up with the intrinsic ability to distinguish instantly between the names 'Benny' and 'Penny'. Because the English language divides the VOT spectrum into two sets of sounds, for example the voiced and voiceless pairs of consonants /b/ versus /p/, /d/ versus /t/, and /g/ versus /k/, children learning English acquire the ability to use their innately specified gift of categorical perception to divide the VOT continuum into two equal halves, corresponding to the voiced and voiceless consonants just exemplified. On the other hand, children exposed to a different language, say Thai, which has three, not two, VOT consonantal contrasts, grow up after years of exposure with the ability to make a three-way categorical split. Thus Thai children rapidly acquire the ability to hear an extremely short VOT as /b/ (as in /bai/, the Thai word for 'leaf'), a slightly longer VOT as /p/ (a sound like the /p/ in the English word 'spring', as in /pai/, the Thai word for 'go'), and any VOT longer than 50 milliseconds as an aspirated /ph/ (a sound very close to the English /p/ and which is used in the Thai word, /phai/, which means 'paddle').

When any language learner, whether a child learning their first language, or an adult a second language, is exposed to the VOT settings of a particular language over an extended period of time with lots of opportunities for acoustic input, it appears that they use their innate ability to hear speech sounds categorically to acquire the appropriate VOT settings. The successful comprehension of speech sounds is, therefore, a combination of the innate ability to recognize fine distinctions between speech sounds which all humans appear to possess, along with the ability all learners have to adjust their acoustic categories to the parameters of the language, or languages, they have been immersed in. We see then that learning to comprehend, like all aspects of language acquisition, is again a merger of both nature and nurture.

The comprehension of words

Sounds represent only a tiny and rather primitive component of comprehension. What about our comprehension of words? What psycholinguistic mechanisms affect lexical processing? Obviously, the comprehension of words is much more complex than the processing of phonemes. Because even short, one-syllable words are made up of at least several sounds, because these sounds may be written in different and inconsistent ways in various languages, because there are literally tens of thousands of words in the vocabulary of any language (in contrast to a few score phonemes), and, most importantly of all, because they convey meanings, the comprehension of words is indeed a very complex psycholinguistic process.

One model that psycholinguists have adopted to account for this complexity is **Parallel Distributed Processing** (**PDP**). Using a model of cognition developed from recent research in neurology, computer science, and psychology, the PDP perspective argues that we use several separate but simultaneous and parallel processes when we try to understand spoken or written language. These processes are used at all levels of linguistic analysis, but play a particularly conspicuous role in the comprehension of words and sentences. One explanation, based on this approach, for how we access the words stored in our mental lexicon is the **logogen** model of comprehension. When you hear a word in a conversation or see it on the printed page (as you have just done with this new term), you stimulate an individual logogen, or lexical detection device, for that word. Logogens can be likened to individual neurons in a gigantic neuronal network; if they are activated, or 'fired', they work in parallel and in concert with many other logogens (or nerve cells) to create comprehension. High-frequency words (like the word 'word') are represented by logogens with hair triggers; they are rapidly and frequently fired. Low-frequency words (like the word 'logogen' itself) have very high thresholds of activation and take longer to be incorporated into a system of understanding.

By adopting this model, psycholinguists can account for the comprehension of words in several different ways: in terms of their spelling (for example homophones like 'threw' and 'through', which are spelled differently but pronounced alike); on the basis of their pronunciation (for example homographs like the verb 'lead' and the noun 'lead', which are spelled alike but pronounced differently), or in terms of the grammatical functions that the word might fill (for example 'smell' can function as either a noun or a verb, but 'hear' functions only as a verb and requires derivational or lexical changes, like 'hearing' or 'sound' when used as a noun). Finally, comprehension can be linked via PDP to the network of associations that are triggered by a word's meaning (for example the word 'leaf' can very rapidly evoke images of trees, pages in a book, or even words which sound similar such as the verb 'leave').

A clear example of the usefulness of a PDP approach to the comprehension of words is an experience many of us encounter on an almost daily basis, what psychologists term the **Tip-Of-the-Tongue** (**TOT**) phenomenon. Because our long-term memory storage is better for recognition than for recall, we often know that we know a word so that, even when we can't recall it from our memory, it is on the tip of our tongue, and we can instantly recognize the word when it is presented to us. Psycholinguists have studied this frequent linguistic experience and have discovered several intriguing aspects of the TOT phenomenon. For one thing, the momentarily lost word isn't always completely forgotten; parts of the word are often subject to recall and, most commonly, these remembered fragments are the first letters or the first syllable.

Suppose you are trying to recall an obscure word, say the word which refers to the belief that everything that happens to us has already been ordained by God. If we have actually acquired this word at some time in our life, then we usually have some TOT memory of how it begins. We think that it is a polysyllabic word which begins with 'pre-'. In trying to produce the word, we somewhat frustratedly experience the TOT phenomenon because we know we know the word, and we remember something about the term, but we simply cannot recall it on demand. Another intriguing aspect about examples like this is that although we cannot reproduce the word, we can instantly recognize any words that are <u>not</u> the one we are trying to recall. As soon as we see or hear the following words, we know that none of them is the TOT item we are searching for.

prestidigitation   pretension   Presbyterian   predilection

We know that even though none of these word fits our ephemeral image of the target of our lexical search, they are all pretty good matches. For one thing, the TOT word we are trying to recall seems to end with an '-ion' like the set of terms above. Often we have vague memories of the beginning and the ending of TOT terms but not the middle, which is, so to speak, submerged. This so-called **bathtub effect** allows us to search for words in a dictionary, since memory of the beginning of the missing word allows us to access alphabetical files, and conversely, the memory of how the word ends allows us to use rhyming as one strategy to confirm whether the word we are searching for is among those on the page in front of us. Often, it is through these search strategies that we suddenly come up with the word, or recognize it instantly if it is presented to us. At one moment we have only partial recollection, and at the next we remember the word is 'predestination'.

Notions like logogens and PDP seem to be useful in explaining the TOT phenomenon under discussion here. We were able to recall, at least in this TOT example, the first and the last part of the logogen for the target word, and this allowed us to compare and contrast other words with similar logogens. Notice, too, that we are not confined to one type of comprehension or recognition processing when we are contrasting a TOT word with other possible targets. While we are looking at these words morphologically, we are also making other judgments. In the example above, 'Presbyterian' was rejected because of the capital letter (the word we were trying to retrieve was not a proper noun), and yet at the same time, we might have been dimly aware of a possible semantic connection since this word and our TOT term have something to do with theology while the other words on the list do not. Here our **schematic knowledge**, based on all of our life experiences, assists the lexical search process.

A PDP model of comprehension is able to explain the very rapid and accurate way people make judgments about which, if any, words on a list are a temporarily forgotten TOT word because it accounts for the concurrent use of more general, or top-down, semantic information as well as more detailed, or bottom-up, 'bathtub' knowledge about the phonology or the exact spelling of the item being searched for. This example also demonstrates the effects of **spreading activation networks**. When you first try to recall a TOT word, it seems as if your memory is a complete blank and you have absolutely no clues about the word in question. Nevertheless, the more you think about the missing term and the more you contrast it with similar but not identical words, the more pieces of knowledge you activate so that the network of associations spreads. The first two items on the list, 'prestidigitation', and 'pretension', do not fit the lexical network you have established, but 'Presbyterian' does and, depending on your linguistic and schematic knowledge, even though this third word isn't a match, it helps accelerate the activation of lexical relationships so that eventually the target word you are searching for is reached.

Lexical recognition and comprehension then are much more difficult processes to understand than the recognition of phonemes, but we have learned several things about these processes over the past few decades. First, we know that words are not stored solely in alphabetical order in mental 'dictionaries', although the bathtub effect demonstrates that this type of serial-order recognition and retrieval is available to us. We also store words according to how their last syllables rhyme, for example. Second, we have learned that comprehension is not an absolute state where language users either fully comprehend or are left completely in the dark. Rather, it seems that comprehension involves a dynamic, growing, and active process of searching for relevant relationships in spreading activation networks. The logogen model suggests that familiar words connect rapidly with other nodes in the network; unfamiliar words take time because the connections have not been automated. Finally, we see that people do not rely on one general strategy to comprehend words, but simultaneously use both top-down information involving context and meaning and bottom-up data about the pronunciation and spelling of words to assist them in decoding the words they hear or read. From all this, it is manifest that listening and reading are not 'simple' or 'passive' activities. They require just as much complex and active mental processing as their more physically overt linguistic counterparts, speaking and writing.

The comprehension of sentences

But comprehension involves much more than the decoding of sounds, letters, and lexical meanings; it also involves the untangling of the semantics of sentences. Psycholinguists first began to examine the comprehension of sentences by basing their research on the model of sentence grammar originally proposed by Chomsky in the 1950s. Chomsky's model claimed that all sentences were 'generated' from a **phrase structure** skeleton which was then fleshed out into everyday utterances by a series of transformational rules (hence the term **Transformational-Generative** (**TG**) grammar). In the original version of grammar, these transformations were plenteous and powerful, and they could create many varieties of 'surface structures' by rearranging, deleting, adding, or substituting words which were found in the 'deep structure' of the original PS skeleton. Using this model, psycholinguists immediately became interested in comparing the number of transformations used to derive sentences and the relative difficulty native speakers experienced in comprehending them. They based these early experiments on sentence pairs like the following.

(1) The dog is chasing the cat.
(2) Isn't the cat being chased by the dog?

From the standpoint of TG grammar, (2) is much more complex than (1), not simply because it contains two more words ('n't' and 'by'), but because unlike (1) which corresponds with the underlying PS sentence, (2) has undergone three transformational changes; it has been transformed into a negative, passive, interrogative sentence. Accepting this linguistic analysis for the moment, it is easy to see why psycholinguists thought that pairs of sentences like these might offer insights into the comprehension process. It seems logical that simple 'kernel' sentences like (1) are easier to comprehend and remember than complex sentences like (2).

Psycholinguists who first experimented with this hypothesis called it the **Derivational Theory of Complexity** (**DTC**), because difficulty in comprehension was derived from the number of transformations that were added on to the original phrase structure of the kernel sentence. Several creative experiments were devised in the 1960s to test the DTC. For example, subjects were given a random assortment of sentences like the following and were then asked to recall both the sentence they had just heard and a string of words spoken immediately after the sentence.

(3) The dog is chasing the cat.	bus/green/chair/ apple/etc.
(4) The dog isn't chasing the cat.	car/blue/sofa/ pear/etc.
(5) Is the cat being chased by the dog?	bike/pink/table/ peach/etc.
(6) Isn't the cat being chased by the dog?	train/yellow/stool/ grape/etc.

Researchers hypothesized that since working memory constrains the amount of new linguistic information we hear, and because each sentence got more and more complicated in a very quantifiable way, the subjects would remember fewer and fewer words following each sentence. That is, based on the DTC, it was claimed that (4) was (3) plus an additional transformation (the negative), (5) was (3) plus two additional transformations (the passive and the interrogative), and (6) was (3) with three additional transformations (the negative, the passive, and the interrogative). Accordingly, it was hypothesized that for sentences like (3), subjects would remember several of the words following the initial sentence (perhaps around six), but that for each successive sentence, subjects would remember one fewer word on the list because their working memory would be taxed by additional transformations. Initial experiments like this based on the DTC showed a very broad confirmation of the hypothesis—the number of words remembered at the end of each sentence seemed to correlate inversely with the number of transformations presumably required to generate each of the sample sentences.

Nevertheless, even those original DTC experiments which appeared to support the basic hypothesis, contained within them evidence that all was not well. One disturbing result was that although in general the more transformations a sentence contained, the more difficult it was to process in an experimental situation, there were unexplainable exceptions to this generalization. In one experiment, which simply asked subjects to match kernel sentences listed in a column on the left with their transformed variants in a right-hand column, although the matching took longer for sentences that contained more transformations, there were several exceptions. Sentences like (4) in the examples on the previous page, which had undergone only one transformational change, into the negative, often took just as much time to match as sentences with two or three transformations, as in examples (5) and (6). This seems very odd given that the interrogative and passive transformations, all contained in (6), are much more complicated than the negative rule, which simply adds 'not' after the verb 'is'. The passive rule, on the other hand, is actually a collection of cumbersome transformations with words being added and rearranged in a complicated way. This would lead one to suspect that, all things being equal, sentences in the passive would take much longer to match (or cause greater constraints on memory) than negative sentences, which have undergone only minimal syntactic change. These early warning signals that the DTC was not as straightforward or as insightful as was originally hoped led to further experimentation. Failure to replicate the apparent successes of the early research led to the demise of the DTC by the end of the decade.

One such replication attempted to repeat the study which looked at the reputed effect of the DTC on memory for lists of words, except rather than have the subjects hear the list of words *after* they heard the test sentence, the subjects listened to the words *before* hearing the sentence. When this slight change in protocol was introduced, it was discovered that the grammatical form of each sentence had no effect on the number of words recalled, suggesting that a larger number of transformations in a sentence does not necessarily occupy more space in working memory. Another series of experiments demonstrated that semantics, rather than syntax, seemed to be the main determinant of comprehension difficulty. Thus, in the examples below, passive sentences like (7) took *less* time to process than active sentences like (8) because they were semantically more plausible. In fact, sentences like (8) tended to be remembered as (7) because subjects retained a rough memory of the word order but were reluctant to admit that they heard the highly implausible event described by (8), even though it was an active sentence. Instead, they were quick to claim what they actually heard was the reputedly more 'difficult' but vastly more plausible passive counterpart (7).

(7) The struggling swimmer was rescued by the lifeguard.
(8) The struggling swimmer rescued the lifeguard.

Another way in which semantics seemed to intervene as a more important variable than the DTC was the manner in which any negative sentence seemed to confuse the subjects. As has been already pointed out, the negative in English is a relatively easy syntactic rule, especially in the case of sentences which include the auxiliary 'be': 'not' (or its contracted form, 'n't') is placed right after the verb 'be' turning an affirmative sentence like (7) into its negative equivalent.

'The struggling swimmer wasn't rescued by the lifeguard.'

Contrast this solitary grammatical change with the four operations that are needed to change an active sentence like (9) into its passive equivalent (10): first the subject and object are reversed; second the preposition 'by' is inserted before the original subject;

third the verb 'be' is introduced in the correct tense; and fourth the main verb is converted into its past participle form.

(9) The puppy hid the bone.
(10) The bone was hidden by the puppy.

Despite all of the changes passivization entails, it still seems that negative sentences take more time to comprehend and are more difficult to remember than passives, a finding that further undermines the hypothesis that the DTC plays a significant role in comprehension. This initial finding led to some further psycholinguistic inquiry into the innate difficulty of negatives and showed that negation, especially double or triple negation, is exceedingly difficult to comprehend, despite the fact that grammatically, it is a simple structure in English. As a simple but revealing confirmation of this finding, quickly try to work out whether the following sentence is true or false.

(11) It's not true that Wednesday never comes after a day that's not Tuesday.

Finally, the original linguistic model which psycholinguists had based their early experiments on had already undergone major revisions. Ironically, even as psycholinguists began their series of DTC experiments in the 1960s, Chomsky had already made extensive changes to the primitive version of TG grammar upon which the DTC studies were based. By the time they were being conducted, he had introduced a revision which reduced the number and the power of transformational rules and, concurrently, featured a more prominent role for semantics in his model of grammar. Not surprisingly, he has continued to introduce further revisions in his model so that today there are virtually no transformations at all. Now, some thirty years later, it is generally accepted that transformational rules, especially as they were conceived of several decades ago, are not psycholinguistically relevant.

If transformational complexity does not affect comprehension, what does? Thanks to further experimentation on a wide range of variables, it seems, quite a few factors. For one thing, ambiguity seems to slow down comprehension time, as has been demonstrated by several studies that use **phoneme monitoring** tasks. These sound like some sort of phonological measure, but they are in fact a method psycholinguists use to tap into the process of sentence comprehension. Subjects listen to sentences like the pairs below and are asked to press a button as soon as they hear a /b/ sound. This allows the experimenter to measure the subjects' reaction times between the moment they heard the /b/ and the instant they reacted. The underlying assumption is that sentences which contain more complex information in the clause preceding the target phoneme will create a correspondingly greater lag in reaction time. Notice that in sentences (12) and (14), the words immediately preceding the target sound /b/ are ambiguous; men can 'drill' by using an instrument or by rehearsing marching formations, and 'straw' can refer either to dried grass or to a tube used for sipping liquids. In contrast, sentences (13) and (15) do not use ambiguous words immediately before the target phoneme.

(12) The men started to drill *b*efore they were ordered to do so.
(13) The men started to march *b*efore they were ordered to do so.
(14) The merchant put his straw *b*eside the machine.
(15) The merchant put his oats *b*eside the machine.

Sure enough, the subjects took several tens of milliseconds longer to hit the button when they heard the /b/ for sentences (12) and (14), most probably because of the ambiguity of the words 'drill' and 'straw', which immediately preceded the target sounds. Subjects were significantly faster in responding to the /b/ for sentences (13) and (15), presumably because they did not have to process two different meanings for 'march' and 'oats', the words which they heard just before the target phoneme.

Sample sentences like the ones just cited reveal another important finding in the psycholinguistic investigation of comprehension. Just as words tend to be processed, at least in part, in a linear, 'left-to-right' order, sentences also seem to be understood sequentially so that each new word serves to add to the meaning of the words which immediately preceded it and, at the same time, helps the listener or the reader to anticipate the next word or words which will follow. This form of 'spreading activation' at the sentence level has led some psycholinguists to posit **Automated**

Transition Networks (**ATNs**) which can be used to predict the next word or word sequence at any juncture of a sentence as it is spoken or printed. Attempts to program computers to make predictions using ATNs have met with limited success, and this particular approach is not very popular, largely because it seems too simplistic to explain sentence comprehension on the basis of the single process of sequential prediction. The Parallel Distributed Processing (PDP) model is a more robust alternative, because it suggests the existence of multiple and parallel sequences of psycholinguistic processes, operating concurrently whenever we attempt to understand novel utterances.

But the general tendency for all listeners and readers to make increasingly confident predictions about the meaning of a sentence as it progresses is well-attested in psycholinguistics and is colorfully called **garden-pathing**. One well-documented example of this phenomenon is the way comprehension is temporarily impeded when the listener or reader meanders down the wrong garden path in comprehending a string of words. Consider the following utterance and imagine that you were listening to it for the first time. After the word 'mile', what word or phrase would you expect to hear?

(16) Since Jay always jogs a mile   seems like a short
                                          distance to him.

You probably expected something like 'he' as in 'he is in fairly good shape' rather than the verb 'seems', and this probably temporarily confused you. In fact, you may have scanned the sentence once or twice to see if there was some misprint. Actually, if we adhered to the rules of English punctuation, there should have been a comma after the first verb, 'jogs'. Researchers asked subjects to read sentences like (16) while they measured their rapid eye movements scanning the text using specially designed contact lenses. They found that when the subjects saw the word 'seems', the eye-fixation time was much longer than at any other point in the sentence. On the other hand, when sentences like (16) were slightly modified so as to remove any ambiguity about the direction of the sentence, as in (17), the subjects did not hesitate after the word 'mile'.

(17) Since Jay always jogs a mile this seems like a short distance to him.

Again we see evidence that the linguistic structure of the sentence affects the processing time. When our guesses about which direction a sentence will go are correct, as is normally the case if we know a language well, our comprehension is rapid, but if we choose the wrong path, as is easy to do in a specially designed sentence like (16), our comprehension is disrupted. And what slows us down is the way we expect words to fit together syntactically. Since 'mile' follows 'jogs', it is natural to assume that all the words to this point match the Noun + Verb + Noun pattern we expect for simple sentences and combine to create the initial clause, 'Since Jay always jogs a mile'. But the stranded verb, 'seems' suddenly demonstrates that we chose the wrong path of comprehension. Garden-pathing is such a natural comprehension strategy, we are unaware of it until it is interrupted, as it is unintentionally in poor writing, or intentionally in jokes or psycholinguistic research.

The comprehension of texts

In addition to the research on sounds, words, and sentences, psycholinguists have also examined the way we process texts. What do we remember of a story that has just been told to us or a letter that we have just read? First of all, with the exception of **mnemonists**—people who have a rare and uncanny ability to recall texts that they have heard or read—our memory is rather poor for structure but is comparatively very accurate for content. Earlier, we observed that the subjects in the DTC experiments were somewhat hazy about the grammatical form of the sentences they were asked to remember. Passive sentences tend to be remembered as active ones, but usually not the reverse. That is, our syntactic memory may be vague but it is not haphazard; we tend to remember sentences in a form that is actually simpler than the structure which we originally read or heard. If there is not too long a gap in time, subjects can remember that a sentence like (6), to take just one example, was a negative question, but they usually recall it as an active sentence, 'Isn't the dog chasing the cat?'

The basic content is remembered but not typically the grammar of the sentence. Only when sentences violate our expectations, as in example (8), do we tend to change the meaning into something that more comfortably matches them, like (7). Interestingly enough, even those with supreme memories for texts, the literally one-in-a-million mnemonists, when they finally start to forget the exact wording of a text, might make minor changes in the words or the grammar, but not in the details of the content.

Psycholinguistic research into the comprehension of texts has demonstrated, among other things, that the presence or absence of background information can dramatically affect the way we remember a piece of discourse. In a famous experiment, subjects read a series of paragraphs and, after each reading, they were asked to repeat as much as possible of what they had just read. Read the following example and then try to replicate this study yourself by closing the book and then by attempting to write down as much as possible of what you have just read.

> With hocked gems financing him, our hero bravely defied all scornful laughter that tried to prevent his scheme. Your eyes deceive you, he had said, an egg not a table correctly typifies this unexplored planet. Now three sturdy sisters sought proof, forging along sometimes through calm vastness, yet more often over turbulent peaks and valleys. Days became weeks as many doubters spread fearful rumors about the edge. At last, from nowhere, welcome winged creatures appeared, signifying momentous success.

Not only did you probably experience difficulty in recalling the exact wording and the sequence of sentences in this seemingly incoherent account, you may also have wondered what is was all about. Now give this paragraph to a friend to read and to recall, but before you do so, point out that this is the story of 'Christopher Columbus discovering America'. In the psycholinguistic experiment that contrasted subjects' ability to recall paragraphs like this, those who were given an appropriate title first demonstrated much more accurate recall than those who were not. This suggests that top-down information, which provides general background knowledge about a text, is useful in the comprehension of larger units of language because it helps activate mental associations which then assist in overall comprehension and recall.

Comprehension concluded

Once again we have discovered that an everyday activity that seems to be simple and straightforward is, upon more intensive scrutiny, complex and variable. In the comprehension of speech sounds, we see further evidence that some parts of human language are innate, and do not have to be learned. The perception of major linguistic differences in sounds, such as VOT, is hard-wired into the human brain, and even young children demonstrate the ability to classify very small differences in VOT into one or another phonetic category. This innate ability is extremely useful for children as they grow up hearing their mother tongue, because it allows them to pick up the few significant differences in that particular language and, at the same time, to ignore the many which are insignificant.

The research into the comprehension of words has shown that we are very much affected by context, and that our understanding is both facilitated and complicated by the different pieces of knowledge we possess for each logogen. It is clear from the TOT phenomenon that we have access to a dictionary-like memory for words. We can 'search' for a partially-remembered word by comparing and contrasting other words which share similar specifications. But our knowledge of and about words is much more extensive: the meaning of a word immediately triggers a spreading activation of associations which help us understand it in many different contexts, and may bring other related words to mind.

The grammatical structure of a sentence might initially influence the garden path we choose in trying to understand it, but the greatest influence on sentence comprehension is meaning. We can see this in the experiments with ambiguous sentences because it is clear that ambiguity slows down processing time, but we also observe it in recall. People remember the 'what' that is spoken or written better than the 'how'. Finally, comprehension of larger units of language also indicates the importance of meaning. Texts that fit into a context which we understand and expect are comprehended more quickly and remembered more readily than ones which are presented to us without a context.

It is plain that only a complex model of comprehension like PDP can begin to account for the way readers and listeners comprehend the millions of linguistic messages they receive each day. Psycholinguists have to develop a model of comprehension that successfully integrates all the diverse, yet parallel and simultaneous processes that we have examined in this chapter, and obviously such a model will be exceedingly elaborate. It will have to begin with the innate mechanisms for language that are wired into the human mind. It will have to account for the way in which young children rapidly learn to extricate significant phonemes, words, sentence structures, and phrases from the multitude of sounds and sights that besiege them each day. And ultimately it will have to explain how some sort of executive decision-maker in the mysterious garden of the human mind decides when to continue along one path toward understanding, when to abandon it abruptly for a more fruitful alternative, and how to seek almost always successfully an accurate interpretation of the intended message.

(Text comprehension passage on page 67 from D.J. Dooling and R. Lachman. 1971. 'Effects of comprehension on retention of prose.' *Journal of Experimental Psychology* 88:216–22.)

5
Dissolution: language loss

In many ways, this final chapter on the loss of language and the unworking of the mind is the obverse of Chapter 1, which dealt with how babies acquire their mother tongue. But unfortunately, it is not just the natural progression of the years that can exact its toll on our speech. Dissolution can be caused by an unhappy accident which assaults the language area of our brain, or by a traumatic event in our personal life, or, as researchers are just beginning to discover, even by some unfortunate roll of the genetic dice. The study of abnormalities of speech has provided psycholinguists with several direct insights into the psychology of language, for example the slip of the tongue data reviewed in Chapter 2. Another illustration of this type of inquiry is the large field of Second Language Acquisition (SLA) research, which could be considered a branch of applied psycholinguistics. Here, the errors that non-native speakers make while they are learning a new language have turned out to reveal at least some of the learning processes they employ. So it is no surprise that psycholinguists have found that the dissolution of language, whether due to accident or age, is a rich source of information about how the human mind controls our attempts to communicate.

Neurolinguistics and language loss

The evidence from aphasia

We will begin with the most extensively studied examples of psycholinguistic dissolution, the loss of language due to brain damage. Since the brief comment on Emily Dickinson's poem quoted in Chapter 1, talk about the brain has been avoided in an attempt to focus on the mind and on mental processes. So far we have assumed that mind and brain are relatively distinct and that it would be misleading to consider them psychologically synonymous. However a different perspective would take the other extreme and claim that the mind and brain are one.

Neurolinguistics, an offspring of psycholinguistics, investigates how the human brain creates and processes speech and language. Before we examine the findings of neurolinguistic research, we need to clear up some popular misunderstandings about the human brain and the way it functions. One example is the disproportionate attention devoted to the well-known anatomical fact that human brains have two separate and virtually identical cerebral hemispheres. Biologically, this is an unremarkable piece of information, for this bifurcation is found in all vertebrates and is itself a characteristic of the bilateral symmetry that pervades our living world. However, there exists an unusual enchantment with the brain in our current culture, so that this anatomical condition has prompted a great deal of discussion about 'left brain versus right brain' differences in human behavior. What the media and most people forget is that, anatomically, there are millions of association pathways which connect the left and right hemispheres together so that in *normal* brains any information in either hemisphere is immediately shared with the other. The function of the **corpus callosum** (the largest sheath of association pathways connecting the two hemispheres) is often unknown, ignored, or misunderstood so that nowadays it is often represented as a 'fact' that there are 'left-brained' and 'right-brained' people in the same way that individuals can be left- or right-handed. Misconceptions like these about neurology lead, quite naturally, to misconceptions about the relationship between the brain and mental states or linguistic structures. But in this final chapter, it is time to take a look at the brain and to acknowledge the legitimacy of neurolinguistics as a sub-field of the psycholinguistics of language. Sadly, we learn the most when this precious piece of anatomy is damaged.

We can get an idea about the way the brain controls human speech and language without resorting to an anatomy text or arranging to view a craniotomy. Take your left hand and cup it over your left ear so that the palm of your hand is clapped over your ear hole. You will find that your hand covers most of the left side of your head and that the first two fingers of your hand extend upward almost to the top of your scalp. If you could see the interior surface of your brain lying under your hand (as surgeons would if they had flapped open the left side of your skull to expose the brain in a craniotomy), you would be able to identify, after some scrutiny, two vertical strips of brain tissue running down from the top of your head, roughly the same size and in the same position as the first and second finger of your hand. The more forward strip, the one covered by your middle finger, is called the **motor cortex** and is the primary area of the brain for the initiation of all voluntary muscular movement. The strip just parallel to this, and covered by your index finger, is the **sensory cortex**. This is the primary location for processing all sensations to the brain from the body.

Because our central interest is in language and not in the anatomical mapping of human neurology, we are most concerned with the location of the control of speech organs and the sensation of speech sounds within these two strips. And here, we run into one of the many oddities of our neurological system. It is, in fact, the top part of the brain which controls the lower extremity of the body and vice versa. In an equally counterintuitive manner, the left side of the brain is responsible for the right side of the body and vice versa. It follows that the tops of the motor and sensory cortices take care of the movement and sensation of your feet, and the bottom parts of these two strips are responsible for your head. Returning to the hand-on-the-head illustration, the tips of your first two fingers lie over the area of the brain which controls your feet (your right foot to be specific), and the base of those two fingers, where they meet your palm, cover the motor and sensory areas which control your head, mouth, and throat. Because language is represented for most people in the left hemisphere, the area of the brain which is crucial for the production and comprehension of human language is covered by the spot where your first two fingers join your hand. Because of their importance to linguistic communication, these two locations, motor and sensory, are named after the two nineteenth-century neurologists who first described their unique linguistic functions. The bottom portion of the motor cortex, the area that is slightly more forward and is covered by the base of your middle finger, is called **Broca's area**, named after a French physician, Paul Broca, who also helped coin the term **aphasia**, the loss of speech or language due to brain damage. Just behind this area, at the lower portion of the sensory cortex, the spot covered by the base of your index finger, is **Wernicke's area**, named after Broca's Austrian contemporary, Karl Wernicke.

These discoveries of the location of speech centers in the cerebral cortex well over a century ago also helped to demonstrate that the human brain differs from the brains of most other animals because it was not **equipotential**. For many species, including mammals like rats, much of the brain seems to function holistically; if half a brain is damaged, the animal seems to lose about half of its functions, so approximately any area is equal in potential importance to any other area. Not so with the human brain, as Broca, Wernicke, and other nineteenth-century neurologists discovered and as has been further confirmed and refined by a century of research. One of the first pieces of evidence that certain functions of human behavior were localized and were not diffusely represented throughout the brain was this nineteenth-century discovery that different areas of the brain controlled different language functions. Speech production resided largely in Broca's area and comprehension of language was confined pretty much to Wernicke's area. By localizing specific functions to particular areas, it seems that human brains create more compact and powerful neurological 'computers' than those employed by most other animals, which tend to rely more on the equal potential of any area of their cortex for functional processing.

But like all animals, humans are susceptible to injury, probably even more susceptible than animals when it comes to the central nervous system (the brain and spinal cord). Suppose a friend or relative of yours was unfortunate enough to sustain an injury that just happened to be located in either of these two relatively small areas of the brain straddling the top of your left ear. The damage could arise from a loss of blood supply to that location due to a stroke, or from an invasive injury like an automobile accident or a gunshot wound. There are at least two consequences to misfortunes like these that make the central nervous system unique in relation to any other part of the body. First of all, because there are no pain receptors in the brain, any distress that is felt comes from the tissues that surround the brain, the source of discomfort in a headache, and not the brain itself, and that is why a stroke, unlike a heart attack, is not necessarily a painful experience. The second irony is that of all the tissue that comprises the human body, the nerves in the central nervous system do not regenerate. Once they are damaged, they do not grow back, so brain injury is permanent, though, given the right circumstances, functional loss is sometimes recovered, most frequently within a year of the initial injury.

Let us return now to the consequences of injuries to the two 'language centers' of the brain. There are many different types of aphasia, varying in their degree of severity and the way they might overlap, but the two classic types are representative of this malady. Damage to Broca's area usually affects one or all of the stages of speech production reviewed in Chapter 2. **Broca's aphasia** is characterized by speech and writing which is slow, very hesitant, and in severe cases, completely inhibited. Although automatic speech and function words can remain almost unaffected, usually the production of key words, like subjects, verbs, and objects, is hesitant and inaccurate. Nevertheless, comprehension is relatively spared. If the injury is located in a more posterior position, just to the back of the upper ear, then patients usually experience **Wernicke's aphasia**; speech production and writing are pretty much intact, but because the sensory cortex is damaged, patients experience a great deal of trouble processing linguistic input. Although speech flows more fluently and comfortably than for Broca's aphasics, patients afflicted with Wernicke's aphasia tend to ramble somewhat incoherently. Part of this stems from their inability to process conversational feedback due to the problems they confront in comprehension. Remember that in both types and for most cases, aphasia occurs only if either of these two areas are damaged in the *left* hemisphere of the brain. Broca's and Wernicke's areas are unilateral, and reside only in the left hemisphere, at least for almost all right-handed people. Damage to the parallel areas in the right hemisphere does not normally affect in language production or comprehension, although, as neuropsychologists have discovered, it affects other types of human behavior, for example the correct recall and naming of familiar faces, or the ability to read maps.

A good illustration of the type of language dissolution these two types of aphasia create is found in the following excerpts from speech produced by a Broca's and a Wernicke's patient. Although written transcripts fail to capture many of the features of speech so conspicuous in a tape recording or face-to-face interview, the examples printed below reveal remarkably different patterns of linguistic production for the two patients. The Broca's aphasic struggles to search for appropriate words and ends up producing mostly nouns. He also seems unable to use grammatical function words to string phrases and clauses together, although his intention to communicate is almost painfully apparent. The speech of the Wernicke's patient, on the other hand, appears to be a series of cohesive phrases and clauses, without coherence or apparent communicative purpose.

Broca's aphasia
[The patient is attempting to describe an appointment for dental surgery.]

Yes ... ah ... Monday ... er ... Dad and Peter H ..., and Dad ... er ... hospital ... and ah ...Wednesday ...Wednesday, nine o'clock ... and oh ...Thursday ... ten o'clock, ah doctors ... two ... an' doctors ... and er ... teeth ... yah

Wernicke's aphasia
[The patient is trying to describe a picture of a family in a kitchen.]

Well this is ... mother is away here working her work out o'here to get her better but when she's looking, the two boys looking in the other part. One their small tile into her time here. She's working another time because she's getting too ...

(from H. Goodglass and N. Geschwind. 1976. 'Language disorders (aphasia)' in E. C. Carterette and M. P. Friedman (eds.): *Handbook of Perception: Volume 7. Language and Speech.* Academic Press, pages 389–428)

The surgical evidence

Neurolinguistics has progressed enormously since the nineteenth century, and as a consequence of advances in diagnosis and surgery, the particular sub-field known as **aphasiology** (the study of aphasia, or loss of speech) has flourished especially. Two kinds of surgical operation have a particular bearing on questions of language dissolution. One of these procedures is **hemispherectomy**. In rare cases, when a life-threatening neurological condition is found in either the left or right hemisphere of a patient (for example a rapidly growing malignant tumor), and there is no alternative to surgical treatment, neurosurgeons will open up the affected side of the skull and remove almost the entire left or right hemisphere! This procedure used to be performed even on adults, but now it is fairly much restricted to children under the age of ten. There is a dramatic difference between the effects of this operation on adults and young children when it comes to speech. When an adult undergoes a left hemispherectomy, he or she becomes completely aphasic, except for a few words of automatic speech, and this is why such operations are rarely performed nowadays. Conversely, hemispherectomies performed on young children, quite amazingly, do not lead to loss of speech.

How do we reconcile this neurolinguistic phenomenon with the claims made earlier that language centers are localized to specific areas of the left hemisphere? Certainly, the key factor here is the age of the brain. During the first decade of life, the human brain is continuously evolving and growing. Cognitive and linguistic functions have not yet been localized to specific areas (although these sites appear to be genetically predetermined), and this allows for the **neuroplasticity** of the still maturing brain. When a young brain encounters traumatic injury, even to the extent of losing an entire cerebral hemisphere, because it is still maturing, and because the primary areas of cognitive and linguistic functioning have not undergone **canalization** (established as neuronal networks), a child does not suffer the extensive functional loss that an adult does. Consequently, we can see that the effects of neurological damage on linguistic performance are not strictly predictable from anatomical change. In this case, for example, age is a critical factor.

Does this mean that children are spared all neuropsychological or neurolinguistic disadvantage? Certainly not. Childhood aphasia exists, though it is much less common than its adult counterpart, and congenital language disorders such as autism, to be discussed in a moment, very likely stem from neurological abnormalities. But we can see even after this briefest of excursions into neurolinguistics that it is difficult to forge clear-cut links between the neurology of the brain and the language of the mind.

A second, and better known, surgical procedure which also has neurolinguistic relevance is the **split-brain operation** which was developed in the 1970s to help treat specific and rare cases of severe epilepsy. This ancient affliction is most often caused by discharges in the motor cortex in one hemisphere that are instantly transmitted to the corresponding cortex of the other hemisphere via the corpus callosum. There are certain severe and singular forms of epilepsy which remain unaffected by pharmacological treatment, and split-brain surgery was developed to spare sufferers from the terrible trauma of major seizures. In an operation much less dramatic than a hemispherectomy, the surgeon makes a front-to-back incision along the corpus callosum, severing most of the association pathways which connect the left and right hemisphere. Although this might sound almost as grim as a hemispherectomy, there are actually very few negative consequences to the operation, and this rests largely on the fact that all of our senses are bilaterally represented. Our left eye, for example, is controlled by both hemispheres: the left visual field (everything we see to the left of center) is controlled by the right hemisphere and the right field (everything we see to the right of center) by the left hemisphere. The same is true for the right eye, and so even after the corpus callosum is cut, in normal, everyday situations, information from either eye goes to both hemispheres.

A number of unique neurolinguistic consequences of this surgical operation have been discovered. Most daily functions, including speech and language were found to be unaffected; it was only under experimental conditions that certain strange, linguistic processing constraints emerged. For example, when specially selected words were flashed very rapidly on a screen, normal subjects read them as single words, but these same words were read as only *half* a word by the split-brain patients. Take the following illustration. When the word 'HEART' was flashed to subjects on a screen, with the middle of the word right in the center of the field of vision, normal subjects had no trouble in reading it. When the same word was flashed to split-brain subjects, however, they read only the right half; that is, they claimed they saw just the word 'ART', and seemed to miss completely the 'HE' on the left.

HEART   HE**ART**
[What normal subjects read.]   [What split-brain patients read.]

The discrepancy can be explained by the fact that when a word like 'HEART' is flashed momentarily in front of our eyes, the image does not last long enough for us to read it completely, but we can reconstruct it as one word because our corpus callosum instantly transfers all linguistic information which enters our *right* hemisphere from the left visual field into our *left* hemisphere, the one that contains the language centers which comprehend and produce language. These centers immediately read this linguistic stimulus as one word, 'HEART'.

Under non-experimental conditions, when there is much more than the merest fraction of a second to catch a word, a split-brain patient has time to scan back and forth and ensure that both the right and the left side of the word are caught by the right visual field and hence fed directly to the left or linguistic hemisphere. The word is then read correctly, just as it was by the patient before surgery. But under these experimental conditions, when words are flashed too fleetingly to be scanned, the split-brain patient is confined to reading only half the field of vision, always the right half. Since 'ART' is an English word, and since it is quickly fed from the right visual field directly to the left hemisphere, it is the only word that is comprehended. Because it lies in the left visual field, 'HE' is just as quickly picked up by the right hemisphere, but since the neurological bridge between the two hemispheres has been cut, the lexical information remains trapped in the right hemisphere, which is not as literate as its cerebral twin. But the left side of the brain does not monopolize *all* of language processing; there are secondary or tertiary linguistic areas even in the right hemisphere, so split-brain patients are dimly aware that there is more than just the word 'ART' staring them in the face. When they are asked, however, to point with their left hand to the word they have just read ('ART'), patients usually point to the letters 'HE'. Apparently, they are influenced by the stranded memory of the word, 'HE' that is floating in the periphery of consciousness in the right hemisphere.

What do the split brain studies tell us about neurolinguistic processing? Some of them have been interpreted to the public as support for the left versus right brain duality. They have been viewed as additional evidence that the left brain houses the logical and conscious mind whereas the right brain is home to the intuitive and the unconscious. But it is not very useful to draw such gross generalizations about normal neuropsychological processing from the results of split-brain patients in experimental studies. It is an enormous leap of faith and logic to assume that the inability of patients to fully process a word flashed momentarily on a screen because their corpus callosum has been severed due to severe epilepsy can be generalized to the claim that, in normal people in everyday situations, the right hemisphere is the seat of intuitive, nonconscious thinking.

Research into aphasia, and studies of hemispherectomy and split-brain patients, has given rise to two superficially contradictory claims about the manner in which the brain processes language. On the one hand, there is irrefutable evidence that for the vast majority of adults, the production and comprehension of speech is located in two closely situated but clearly distinct areas of the left hemisphere, Broca's and Wernicke's, and this localization of function is not fully completed until about ten years old. An incidental corollary of this fact is that the exceptions, who number from five to ten percent of any given population, tend to be left-handers. For them, there is a greater probability of language being localized to the right hemisphere or being represented bilaterally. On the other hand, in contrast to these claims about the neurolinguistic primacy of the left hemisphere, research in all areas of language dissolution shows that human linguistic ability does not *solely* reside in these two relatively small areas on one side of the brain. The left-handed exceptions just cited are a singular counter-example. But even for the preponderance of people, who are right-handed, more and more evidence has implicated the role of secondary and even tertiary areas of speech processing. The 'HEART' example described above provides support for this.

These two findings alone are enough to call into question the validity of neuropsychological models which neatly map various human behaviors on to the brain like a modern version of phrenology, the belief, popular in the nineteenth century, that the configurations of the skull's surface indicated the presence of different emotions. They suggest, instead, that models which use the analogy of a hologram might be more representative of how the human brain works. Holography is a modern form of photography which uses lasers to mold thousands of holograms together to create a rough, but identifiable, three-dimensional picture of an object. Each hologram, or individual cell, in that picture has the potential to depict the entire picture. In other words, holography creates a single picture from many individual depictions of the original. Genuine 'neurolinguistic programming' seems to work in the same way. There are primary locations in the brain for all complex human activities such as language; nevertheless, at the same time, language is diffusely represented in several other locations as well. The holographic metaphor also helps explain why neuroplasticity is lost. The different areas of the young brain can be neurologically programmed to fulfill a variety of functions, but as the child's environment and experience grow in complexity, these various functions are localized to allow for a more efficient allocation of neurological tissue. At about the onset of puberty, as the child enters an adult world, neuroplasticity is lost because localization is complete. But, like the hologram which is both one picture and many, the overall control of language and speech is both localized and diffuse.

Speech and language disorders

Dissolution from non-damaged brains

Up to this point, we have been discussing examples of language dissolution that are the result of operations on the brain, but these cases are rare when compared to the many ways in which an individual's language can deviate significantly from social norms. Their number is too vast to summarize adequately here, but a brief review of two representative examples, stuttering and autism, will help to reinforce several themes and insights that have been brought out earlier in this book.

Stuttering, also referred to as stammering, is one of the most common articulation problems encountered by speech pathologists, at least in most English-speaking countries. Like the slips of the tongue reviewed in Chapter 3, stuttering reveals psycholinguistic information about how speech is organized and planned. Research has demonstrated, first of all, that stuttering is not random: it does not punctuate our speaking spasmodically, like a hiccough. It occurs, most frequently on the initial word of a clause, the first syllable of a word, the initial consonant of a syllable, and on stop consonants (like /p/, /t/, /k/). There is an enormous and somewhat controversial research literature on the causes of stuttering, and explanations range between two classic psycholinguistic extremes.

On the one hand, the **Johnson theory** represents the extreme behavioral view and claims that stuttering originates from traumatic events occurring in early childhood when overly sensitive parents (who often themselves were childhood stutterers) and/or primary school teachers are too assiduous in attempting to ensure that the child speaks fluently. Because language is such a fundamental component of human socialization, caretakers often display disproportionate attention to a child's speech compared to any other aspect of its development. The same parent or teacher who criticizes a four-year-old for blurting out 'P-p-p-please!' is unlikely to comment on the child's less than perfectly coordinated way of walking, for example.

The opposite extreme of this behavioral explanation (which, as might be imagined, has never been much appreciated by either parents or teachers!) is an equally long-standing neurological explanation. The **Orton/Travis theory** states that stammering is caused by the absence of unambiguous lateralization of speech to the left hemisphere. Recall that roughly five per cent of the population (about half of all left-handers) are probably *right* hemisphere dominant for speech and that another two point five per cent (about a quarter of the left-handed population with a few right-handers thrown in) probably has *neither* side of the brain dominant for language and speech. According to this neurologically based explanation, this latter group of exceptional children often become stutterers, largely because the brain lacks a fully established primary language center and is therefore indecisive about how to initiate speech.

Both of these clearly contrasting views use the same statistics for support. Stuttering is usually stereotyped as more characteristic of boys than girls, of left-handers than right-handers, and is seen to run in families. The Johnson theory explains these demographics in the following manner. Since caretakers and primary-school teachers are usually women, and since girls usually supersede boys in linguistic ability at an early age, boys' speech receives more of the inordinate attention and criticism that fosters frustration and stuttering behavior. As they strive to cope with the difficult task of learning their mother tongue, left-handed boys are a minority that are especially singled out and receive excessive attention among all children. The Johnson theory also tries to account for why stammering tends to run in families. Parents and teachers who grew up in families of stutterers, or who stuttered themselves as children, are more apprehensive of their own children, or pupils, growing up with this disability. But the very same evidence is used to account for the Orton/Travis theory. Why boys? In some recent neurological experiments with rats, it was found that atypically high amounts of testosterone can sometimes decrease the chances that some aspect of behavior will get lateralized to one hemisphere or the other, hence the possibility that the bilateral representation of language will occur more frequently in boys than in girls. Why left-handers? For both sexes, about half of all left-handers do not have language represented in the left-hemisphere, and about a quarter of all left-handers have bilateral control for speech. And why does stammering run in families? This may be because there is a genetic component to its origins. For example, it could be similar to color-blindness, which appears most frequently among males but is passed down genetically via the mother.

There are many weaknesses in both of these extreme positions. Perhaps the most telling criticism is that the stereotypes just described are inaccurate. For example there is little statistically significant support for the notion that stuttering is disproportionately represented in left-handed boys. Over the decades since the promulgation of the Johnson and Orton/Travis theories, there has been increasing evidence that it is a complex disorder that varies not only among individuals, but is also highly dependent on situational differences. Most experts believe it derives from the complex interplay of both neurological and environmental causes and can be reduced or cured with treatments which include the use of delayed auditory feedback, behavior modification, music and rhythm, or even medication. In one manifestation or another, all of this work can be viewed as applied psycholinguistics, for it not only attempts to account for the way the mind can control or miscontrol speech, it also tries to apply this knowledge to rectify problems.

All of this raises an extremely important point, one that pervades every aspect of the psychology of language. Language is not solely individual behavior: it is intricately interwoven into the norms, beliefs, and expectations of *society*, and these serve to define what is perceived as 'normal' or 'abnormal' linguistic behavior. So it is with stuttering. Though there is some indication that stuttering universally affects about one per cent of any population of people, the percentage of stuttering varies from country to country, as diagnosed by social institutions like schools. Even between countries which share a language, like Britain and the United States, speech behavior can be interpreted differently because of contrasting social expectations. A moderate amount of stammering in an older man, especially an academic, is completely acceptable in England, but this same behavior is viewed as a borderline speech disorder in America. One does not have to look at brains or to caretakers to see that, for many language disorders, the disability is not just in the mouth of the speaker but it is also framed by the ears of the listeners.

Another disability that is fairly well-recognized though, fortunately, much less common, is **autism**. Like that of stuttering, its cause has long been disputed by opposing camps, who have argued for either behavioral or neurological origins, with the latter receiving the most recent support. But like the research into stuttering, the more we study autism, the more we see that there are several types, and the severity of the disability also varies considerably. Unlike stuttering, however, it is not simply a language impairment, and the first signs of this disorder are apparent in infants, before speech has really developed. An autistic infant exhibits a bizarre disregard for human interaction and, in contrast to a normal child, ignores eye and face contact. Perhaps because this condition creates a lack of social interaction and early communicative bonding, the autistic infant quickly lags behind in achieving the natural milestones of speech production, and within a year or two, the significance of the disease becomes conspicuous. This fundamental inability to bond with people, coupled with the linguistic consequences of this constraint, creates a behavioral pathology severe enough to be labeled a psychosis. In fact, autism is often referred to as childhood schizophrenia.

Language loss arising from inherited disorders

It is now popular to suggest a genetic basis for many forms of human behavior. Genetics should be used as a court of last resort, not as the first line of defense, but recent work in psycholinguistics has uncovered certain rare examples of how language dissolution appears to be inherited. In these cases, which are mercifully rare, we have the truly curious situation where the genes which carry the human heritage for speech are countermanded by an inherited defect that is transported by the same genetic code. With one exception, these inherited disabilities do not attack language directly; loss of linguistic capacity is a consequence of the more global loss of all higher cognitive functions. The least rare of these disabilities is **Down's syndrome**, a disorder that occurs about once in every 600 births and, along with marked anatomical abnormalities, leaves the child moderately to severely impaired in all cognitive functions. The degree of language disability is directly proportionate to the amount of cognitive damage, and there are cases of less severely afflicted children not only acquiring their mother tongue, but learning a second language as well. The enlargement of the tongue in Down's syndrome creates poor articulation, and though comprehension is not significantly affected, expressive speech is hesitant and limited, in a manner reminiscent of Broca's aphasia.

Language loss through aging

There is a humorous birthday card which reads on the front 'Congratulations! You have reached the age when anything goes!', and then listed inside are 'Hearing, Eyesight, Memory, Hair, etc.'. Though the humor expressed might diminish proportionally with the age of the card's recipient, it is true that a reduction in physical and mental abilities often does accompany the aging process. In a slightly more specific way, Jaques' famed soliloquy in *As You Like It,* quoted in Chapter 1, echoes the same sentiment. As we progress through our 'seven ages', in some ways we approach again the condition of the infant we once were, with our 'big manly voice turning again toward childish treble'. As we have already seen in this chapter, various afflictions, neurological, environmental, or hereditary, mean that humans sometimes have the gift of language taken away from them prematurely and unnaturally. As we gradually progress through Shakespeare's seven stages, however, many of the rest of us reach a point when speech is denied us as part of the natural process of aging. Maybe it is on account of our fascination with youth and the future potential it symbolizes, but the study of language dissolution among older people has been practically ignored by psycholinguists. Compared to the massive number of studies conducted on all aspects of first language acquisition, there is a significant lack of psycholinguistic research on language dissolution among the aged. This is particularly unfortunate considering the ever-increasing size of our older populations and the potential revelations such investigations might furnish for the psychology of language. Most assuredly, this is one area of psycholinguistics that should, and probably will, receive more attention in the future. We might begin by asking, was Shakespeare right? Does language loss due to aging recapitulate in reverse order the stages of language acquisition we reviewed in Chapter 2?

The most conspicuous faculty eroded by the aging process is memory, and since language represents a major component of **Long Term Memory (LTM)**, it is inevitable that linguistic performance is adversely affected by any form of significant deficit in LTM. But here as in any other aspect in the study of human behavior, we must guard against anecdotal overgeneralizations. As people grow older, they often complain about difficulty with recalling names, and they perpetually attribute this deficiency to growing old. But the more plausible explanation for this problem is that a sixty-year-old knows considerably more people and more facts than a sixteen-year-old, and since access to LTM is capacity limited, it is more logical to assume that the more you have to remember, the easier it is to forget.

One large study of people's ability to remember fifteen words on a grocery list found that up to the age of fifty, LTM *improved* slightly, but after the fifth decade, subjects typically forgot one item for every successive decade of life. This loss is not as profound as is commonly believed; the same study found that when the participants were asked to recall the list after a forty minute delay, there was no difference between the younger and older subjects in their LTM ability. Contrary to popular conjecture then, it appears that the aged retain about as good an LTM as young people. The memory constraints that may become evident as we get older seem to be due primarily to **Short Term Memory** (**STM**) constraints, or limitations on inputting and accessing the material to be recalled. No definitive research has been undertaken on the effects, if any, of the aging process on specific aspects of language, such as phonology or syntax, but the little evidence just reviewed on the impact of aging on lexical recall indicates that language remains remarkably robust, even in the face of the natural decline that accompanies the loss of physical and mental abilities. Remember, too, that we cannot measure aging directly by chronological years; geriatrics has long taught us that age is more directly a manifestation of health than of the calendar.

This is evident from the occurrence of **Alzheimer's disease** which affects millions of individuals each year. For as yet undetermined reasons which appear to involve both hereditary and environmental factors, the brain of an AD patient deteriorates prematurely, and this loss has profound and ultimately injurious effects on every aspect of a person's performance. Again, serious psycholinguistic study of AD has just begun, but the research which has been undertaken shows that speech and language are not affected in isolation. Linguistic functions gradually disintegrate together with those of emotion, cognition, and personality. A recent study of the written language of older people concluded that those who wrote more complex compositions (i.e. who used more subordination in their sentences) seemed to have a much better chance of not succumbing to AD compared to those who used simpler sentence structures. Correlational studies like this must be interpreted cautiously. The data most probably means that the same cognitive development that promotes writing complexity makes a person less susceptible to AD. It should certainly not be interpreted to mean that classes in advanced composition will develop immunity to this terrible illness.

Often in psycholinguistics, research in another language offers fresh and valuable information in an area of psycholinguistics that is not directly accessed by the linguistic structures of English. Such is the case with some outstanding work by Japanese researchers in neurolinguistics and AD. The Japanese writing system is notably complicated, consisting, for the most part, of two very separate orthographies: *kana*, which are syllabic spellings (IOU for 'I owe you' would be a rough equivalent), and *kanji*, which are ideographs borrowed from Chinese. When literacy tests were conducted on Japanese AD patients, investigators discovered that while the reading and writing of *kanji* was drastically impaired, these skills were quite well preserved when applied to *kana*, at least in the initial stages of AD. Again, the evidence suggests that language is no different from other aspects of human behavior; the more complex the endeavor (in this case, the processing of *kanji*), the greater the degree of affliction from the disease.

Concluding summary

What do all these examples of speech dissolution tell us about the nature of language and mind? Well, for one thing, given the unbelievable complexity of human language, it is quite astounding to realize that among the world's more than five billion speakers, only a remarkably small number of them are afflicted with any of the communicative anomalies reviewed in this chapter. When we consider the intricacy of acquisition, production, and comprehension involved in just one language, our mother tongue, and then add to this the fact that nearly half the world's population are bidialectal if not bilingual, and are able to process two distinct varieties of language successfully, it is amazing that dissolution is a comparative rarity and not the norm. So the first thing we learn from all of these studies of aberrant language is that because they are abnormal, the everyday use of language without disorders in acquisition, production, or comprehension is a wonder of miraculous proportions.

Second, we can acknowledge from the neurological examples which were reviewed in this chapter that there is strong evidence, from the way the brain processes information, for the unique independence of language. In all varieties of aphasia and in many of the neurolinguistic studies of patients who have undergone major brain surgery, it is plain that language and speech enjoy a unique neurological status in the human brain, and we find support for the notion that the capacity to comprehend and produce language is hard-wired to the mid-central area of the left hemisphere for most adults. At the same time, evidence was presented to indicate that speech and language are not always narrowly and immutably localized to one area of the brain. For young children especially, language seems to be more diffusely controlled by both hemispheres. Indeed, one area of neurolinguistics that needs to be more fully examined is how and why language shifts from a broader, bilateral representation in young children to a narrower, unilateral control in adolescents and adults. An even more intriguing puzzle remaining to be solved is why the neurolinguistic evidence tends to support the independence of speech and language from other aspects of behavior, whereas the psycholinguistic data suggests just the opposite—that language is part and parcel of cognition and perception.

When we turn to examples of dissolution that do not seem to be caused by brain damage, we discover, that the data from research on speech and hearing disorders does not differ significantly from the information we have on normal development. The study of stuttering, for example, endorses the notion that the formulation stage is an important level of speech production. But in general, all of these disabilities, irrespective of their origins, whether behavioral, as in stuttering, or clearly genetic, as in DS, or the natural forces of maturation, as in aging, or due to a still unknown combination of forces, such as autism, point to the third and most significant conclusion. By and large, language seems to be closely related to other aspects of human behavior, particularly to cognition.

In summary, the disruptions in the environment or in the genetic code that bring about speech and language disabilities never seem to single out language: they affect linguistic communication because they afflict cognition and perception as a whole. For this reason, psycholinguistics is drawn by language into a more general inquiry of the workings of the human mind.

Readings

Chapter 1
Introduction

Text 1

DANNY STEINBERG: *An Introduction to Psycholinguistics*:
Longman 1993, pages 45–6

Chapter 1 makes the claim that speech and language are a 'uniquely human possession'. In his review of the failed attempts to teach human languages (like ASL) to apes, Steinberg encourages us to question why we appear to be a linguistically unique species.

The research with animals clearly shows that animals have only a rudimentary language ability, whether in the wild or through training. What is puzzling and requires explanation is why their language ability is so low when their overall intellectual ability is so much higher. Apes exhibit, for example, intelligent complex behavior regarding social organization, food acquisition, and problem solving. Why, then, are they not able to learn more of the sign language taught to them? After all, human children learn sign language in all of its complexity. And why couldn't they at least learn to understand human speech given that they have a hearing acuity which is as good or better than human hearing? After all, there are human beings who are born without the ability for speech production, yet they can learn to understand human language in all of its complexity. ...

Contemporary theorists basically offer two types of explanation on the issue of animals vs. humans in the acquisition of language. Piaget, Putnam and other empiricists hold that animals lack certain aspects of general intelligence which are needed for learning complex language. Chomsky, on the other hand, argues that the effect is due to animals being born without a special language ability, an ability that is little related to intelligence. Whether animals lack intelligence or lack a special language ability is related to the fundamental issue of how human beings, themselves, acquire language. Do we acquire language through intelligence or through a special language ability? Despite much argument, dispute and even a little objective inquiry, this question as yet remains unresolved. In any case, whether it be special intelligence or a special innate language ability, it seems evident that animals do not have it.

▷ *As Steinberg observes, the difference between apes and children does not seem to be intelligence or in the ability to hear. To rephrase his initial question then, why do you think children can learn human sign language, whereas experiments to teach sign language to apes have, for the most part, failed?*

▷ *Steinberg introduces two possible explanations for the unique ability of all humans to acquire language. Which sounds most plausible to you as the key criterion—intelligence or a special language ability?*

▷ *The role of environment is not mentioned in this discussion. In what way(s) might the differences between the environments in which animals and children are born and raised influence the acquisition of language?*

Text 2

LEV VYGOTSKY: 'Thought and speech' in Sol Saporta (ed.): *Psycholinguistics: A Book of Readings*. Holt, Rinehart & Winston 1961, page 519

One of the first psychologists to think about the psychology of language was Vygotsky, whose writings in the late 1930s have been translated from his native Russian. Vygotsky claimed that language had both an external and an internal form, and it was the latter that could provide the clearest window to thought.

The correct understanding of inner speech must be based on the assumption that it represents a specific whole with its own laws and complicated relationships to other forms of speech activity. To investigate the relations of inner speech to thought on the one hand, and to words on the other, we must first determine its specific characteristics and its special function. It makes a great difference whether I speak to myself or to other persons. Inner speech is speech for oneself. External speech is for others. It cannot be supposed even for a moment that such a fundamental distinction will have no consequences for the structure of both kinds of speech. The absence of vocalization is, in itself, only a consequence of the specific nature of inner speech. Inner speech is not what precedes external speech or reproduces it in memory, but that which is opposed to external speech. External speech is the turning of thoughts into words, its materialization and objectification. With inner speech it is a reverse process—speech turns into thought. Therefore their structures must be different.

▷ *Vygotsky holds that most inner speech is silent and unvocalized and that it creates thinking, not the other way around. What are some differences between 'speaking to oneself' or 'speaking to others'?*

▷ *If 'inner speech turns into thought', can there be thought without language?*

Chapter 2
Acquisition: when I was a child, I spoke as a child

Text 3
ANNE FERNALD: 'Human maternal vocalizations to infants as biologically relevant signals: an evolutionary perspective' in Paul Bloom (ed.): *Language Acquisition: Core Readings.* MIT Press 1994, page 71

As noted in the beginning of Chapter 2, although all normal babies go through the stages of crying, cooing, and babbling, they do not do so in a vacuum. Social interaction, especially with the primary caretaker, plays a vital role, as demonstrated here in Fernald's summary of research on the language mothers direct to infants.

Four major findings emerge from these studies on infants' responsiveness to affective vocal expressions. First, at the age of five months, when infants are not yet showing consistent selective responsiveness to positive and negative facial expressions, infants do respond differentially to positive and negative vocal expressions, suggesting that the voice is more powerful than the face as a social signal in early infancy. Second, infants respond with appropriate affect to positive and negative vocal expressions, smiling more to Approvals than to Prohibitions. Third, infants are more responsive to affective vocalizations in ID [infant-directed] speech than in AD [adult-directed] speech, suggesting that the exaggerated prosodic characteristics of maternal vocalizations to infants increase their salience as vocal signals. And finally, young infants are responsive to affective vocalizations spoken with infant-directed prosody even in languages that they have never heard before, providing evidence for the functional equivalence of such ID vocalizations across cultures. These findings indicate that the melodies of mothers' speech are compelling auditory stimuli, which are particularly effective in eliciting emotion in preverbal infants.

The finding that American infants differentiate maternal vocalizations in some but not all languages suggests that cultural differences in the nature and extent of emotional expressiveness may also have an early influence on infants' responsiveness to vocal signals. A process of early cultural 'calibration' might account for these cross-language differences. According to this explanation, infants in all cultures are initially responsive to the same vocal cues, that they find smooth, wide-ranging pitch contours of moderate loudness to be pleasing, while they find low, narrow pitch contours that are short, staccato, and loud to be more aversive. However, cultural differences in display rules governing emotional expression may determine the levels and range of emotional intensity to which the infant is routinely exposed and which the infant comes to expect in social interaction with adults.

▷ *If the responses of babies are largely molded by their mother's voices, how might this explain the rapid emergence of the child's mother tongue beginning at the babbling stage of around six months?*

▷ *Like other developmental psycholinguists, Fernald describes the ID speech used by mothers as highly exaggerated in intonation and in affective (emotional) content. What are some advantages of ID speech over AD speech from the perspective of the language-learning infant?*

Text 4

LILA GLEITMAN and ELISSA NEWPORT: 'The invention of language by children: environmental and biological influences on the acquisition of language' in Daniel Osherson (ed.): *Language: An Introduction to Cognitive Science*. The MIT Press 1995, page 21

Since particular languages are examples of language in general, their specific features are related to universal ones which characterize language as a generic human endowment. Gleitman and Newport here describe how such universals play an important role in enabling children to learn their mother tongue successfully.

The universality of language is, moreover, no quirk or back corner of human mentality but rather one of the central cognitive properties whose possession makes us truly human. If we humans ever get to another planet and find organisms who speak like us, it is likely that we will feel some strong impetus to get to know them and understand them—rather than trying to herd them or milk them—even if they look like cows.

While we have emphasized the biological underpinnings of language acquisition, we must also repeat that part of the normal acquisition process clearly involves learning from the environment as well: English children learn English, not Greek or Urdu. The surface manifestations of human languages are marvelously variable, and children learn whichever of these manifestations they are presented with (as long as what they hear is organized in accord with the general principles of human language, and as long as it is presented at the proper maturational moment).

Language acquisition is therefore a complex interaction between the child's innate capacities and the social, cognitive, and linguistic supports provided in the environment. What we have tried to emphasize, however, is that acknowledgment of significant environmentally caused variation should not blind us to the pervasive commonalities among all languages and among all their learners. Specific languages are apparently acquired within the constraints of a specialized and highly evolved biological endowment, which learns languages only in particular ways and only at particular moments of life.

▷ *The authors mention two environmental constraints on child language acquisition: hearing and appropriate maturation. Can you think of other environmental constraints on normal language learning?*

▷ *Reference is made in this text to the way the child's innate capacities are supported by factors in its environment. How is this consistent with the points made in Text 3 about the child's response to vocal expressions?*

Text 5

PAUL BLOOM: 'Overview: controversies in language acquisition' in Paul Bloom (ed.): *Language Acquisition: Core Readings*. MIT Press 1994, page 11

When children acquire language they do not only learn its grammar but its lexis—the specific meanings which are encoded in its vocabulary (and which would seem to be especially subject to environmental factors). Bloom challenges us to deliberate on how children manage to do this.

Perhaps the deepest mystery in the study of language acquisition is how children come to learn the meanings of words. Although there is considerable theoretical and empirical work on this topic, we have little understanding of how the process takes place. This might have to do with the nature of this problem; while syntax and phonology can be argued to be 'closed' or 'modular' systems, the same cannot be true of word meaning. An adequate theory of how children learn the meaning of words such as 'dogs' and 'giving' requires some account of what it is to possess the corresponding concepts of DOGS and GIVING—which might in turn involve nothing less than a full-blown theory of human cognition. ...

As a starting point, many investigators have construed the process of word learning as hypothesis formation and testing. The adult uses a new word, the child notes the context in which the word is used, and formulates a hypothesis concerning the concept to which the word corresponds. Further instances where the word is used cause the child to strengthen, modify, or reject this initial hypothesis.

▷ *It is possible that children are born with the innate knowledge that languages follow certain* grammatical *principles, but their acquisition of* words *depends crucially on their environment. What are some semantic features of 'dogs' which collectively would help the language-learning child to associate this term only with this animal and no others?*

▷ *Imagine that you are a child, trying to learn a new word like 'dog'. What hypotheses might you create to distinguish animals called 'dogs' from those called 'cats'?*

Text 6

JEAN BERKO (GLEASON): 'The child's learning of English morphology' in Sol Saporta (ed.): *Psycholinguistics: A Book of Readings.* Holt, Rinehart & Winston 1961, page 371

Berko is summarizing her seminal experiment on the ability of young children to use grammatical endings (like plural and past tense) correctly on nonsense words—for example, their ability to produce 'wugs' (pronouncing the final /s/ with the /z/ sound) as the correct plural pronunciation of the singular form 'wug'.

If knowledge of English consisted of no more than the storing up of many memorized words, the child might be expected to refuse to answer our questions on the grounds that he had never heard of a *wug, for instance, and could not possibly give us the plural form since no one had ever told him what it was. This was decidedly not the case. The children answered the questions; in some instances they pronounced the inflexional endings they had added with exaggerated care, so that it was obvious that they understood the problem and wanted no mistake made about their solution. Sometimes, they said, 'That's a hard one,' and pondered a while before answering, or answered with one form and then corrected themselves. The answers were not always right so far as English is concerned; but they were consistent and orderly answers, and they demonstrated that there can be no doubt that children in this age range [six years old] operated with clearly delimited morphological rules.

▷ *The children in Berko's experiment were not at all confused when presented with strange words they had never heard before. What does this suggest about the way young children acquire the vocabulary of their mother tongue?*

▷ *It is sometimes claimed that children pick up their mother tongue effortlessly and unconsciously. How does this square with Berko's observations about the reflective answers given by some of the children?*

Chapter 3
Production: putting words in one's mouth

Text 7
STEVEN PINKER: 'Why the child holded the baby rabbits: a case study in language acquisition' in Daniel Osherson (ed.): *Language: An Invitation to Cognitive Science*. MIT Press 1995, page 107

One of the points repeatedly made by generative linguists is that the learning of grammar rules provides for the production of an infinite number of novel sentences which have never been encountered before. Pinker here emphasizes the unpredictable creativity of linguistic production.

Human language is one of the wonders of the natural world. Unlike other species' calls and cries, which convey a fixed set of messages—such as warnings of danger of claims to territory—the noises that come out of our mouths can convey an unlimited number of different, precise, structured, brand-new propositions. I can put together sentences that can tell you anything from how to build a small thermonuclear device in your basement, to the mating habits of the octopus, to the latest twists in your favorite soap opera plot. You would have never heard these sentences before, but you would recognize them as English and understand their meanings. The number of sentences that a human can produce and understand is astonishing—a hundred million trillion different sentences twenty words or less, according to one estimate. Indeed, a person is capable, in principle, of producing an *infinite* number of sentences (putting aside the fact all humans are mortal). By the same logic that allows us to say that there are an infinite number of numbers (if you ever think you have listed them all, I can create a new one by adding 1 to the largest), there are an infinite number of sentences; if you ever think you have listed them all, I can create a new one by adding *He wrote that ...* to the longest.

▷ *With reference to this text and Text 5, do you think that the ability to put sentences together necessarily means that they can be understood? Is the production of sentences all that is involved in language acquisition or use?*

Text 8

ANN M. PETERS: *The Units of Language Acquisition.*
Cambridge University Press 1983, page 2

Linguists analyse language in terms of phonological, grammatical, and lexical forms. But these units of descriptive analysis may not be the same as units of acquisition or use. Ann Peters suggests that language may also be internalized as larger chunks or formulas.

Relatively little linguistic research has been done to identify the actual units from which mature speakers construct utterances. The focus has rather been on describing only the corpus of utterances themselves (the 'language') in the most economical and nonredundant terms, regardless of how they were produced. Descriptions of adult, and in fact also child, language therefore strive to minimize both the number and size of the basic distinctive units used. Thus one looks for distinctive features in phonology, and morphemes in syntax, rather than functional units as measured, for instance, by occurrence of invariant combinations, fluency of production, or characteristic intonation contours. ...

If this model of language is taken also as an accurate model of the adult speaker, it implies that the speaker stores the lexicon and grammar in the most nonredundant form and produces each utterance afresh from the minimal units. Evidence has been accumulating, however, that normal adult speakers actually store and call into play entire phrases that may be many words long—phrases that are not constructed from their ultimate grammatical constituents each time they are used. Accordingly, while words and morphemes may be the ultimate units in a logical and economical description of language, the actual units used in speech production may be different. ...

In what follows, I will use the term 'speech formula' to mean a multi-morphemic phrase or sentence that, either through social negotiation or through individual evolution, has become available to a speaker as a single prefabricated item in her or his lexicon. Not only are such formulas fixed in structure; they also tend to be rather strongly situationally conditioned. They range from memorized sequences (such as counting, the alphabet, nursery rhymes), through swear phrases (*goddammit*), exclamations (*oh boy*), greeting and leave-taking rituals (*how are you, see you*), social control phrases (*lookit, my turn, shut up*), to idioms (*kick the bucket*) and small talk (*isn't it a lovely day*).

▷ *Can you give examples of speech formulas in your own language? Does your own experience tell you that they are indeed stored ready for use as this author suggests?*

▷ *What do you think the author means when she says that prefrabricated phrases have become available through 'social negotiation' or 'individual evolution'?*

▷ *How far does the view expressed here about the construction of utterances correspond with Pinker's account in Text 7 of the productivity of language?*

Text 9
VICTORIA FROMKIN: 'Speech production' in Jean Gleason and Nan Ratner (eds.): *Psycholinguistics*. Harcourt, Brace, Jovanovich 1993, page 276

Like the two preceding texts, this one deals with the issue of how language is produced from linguistic items in mental storage. Again, the question is: what items are stored, and how are they put together in the production process?

When we produce an utterance corresponding to some thought we wish to convey, we cannot go to a mental storage unit and pull out the appropriate stored message. The brain's finite storage capacity cannot warehouse an infinite set of utterances, and most of what we say has never been said in just that way before. Thus, speech is produced by stringing together, arranging and rearranging a limited number of stored items. A major question in trying to understand the production process is to determine the size and nature of these units. Even a long memorized passage, such as the *Gettysburg Address* or *Mary Had a Little Lamb*, must be mentally represented by its constituent parts including sentences, clauses, phrases, words, morphemes, syllables, phonemes, and even phonological features, since, as we will see below, all of these units represent items which may be disordered or forgotten or remembered as fragments. As this chapter will explore, these units of language, which linguists use in describing the structure of language, have been shown to be just those discrete units out of which the semicontinuous physical speech signal is composed during the process of speech production.

▷ *The author says (at the end of this passage) that the units of linguistic description are the same as the units of language production. How does this view relate to that of Peters in Text 8?*

Text 10

KATHRYN BLOCK and WILLEM LEVELT: 'Language production: grammatical encoding' in Morton Ann Gernsbacher (ed.): *Handbook of Psycholinguistics*. Academic Press 1994, page 954

In speech production is is quite common for speakers to make errors in finding the word they want from their mental lexicon. The word as a linguistic unit, or lemma, may, for example, call up different lexical concepts. This passage points out how errors occur at the conceptual and lemma levels of the mental lexicon.

There are three major kinds of lexical selection errors, called sub-stitutions, blends, and exchanges. In all three cases a nontarget lemma is activated and an incorrect word form is produced. But there are different ways in which this derailing activation can come about. Consider examples ... of substitutions.

(1) ... *carrying a bag of cherries. I mean grapes* (Stemberger, 1985)

(2) *He's a high–low grader* (Fromkin, 1973)

(3) *Get out of the clark* [intended: *car*] (Harley, 1984)

(4) *A branch falling on the tree* [intended: *roof*] (Fromkin, 1973) ...

One potential cause of a substitution error is that an alternative lexical concept is activated along with the target. In (1) the speaker intended to express the notion GRAPE, but CHERRY was activated at the same time. This may result from activation spreading at the conceptual level. Because GRAPE and CHERRY are semantically related (both are small round fruits), there is some linkage between them in the conceptual network. If both lexical concepts then activate their lemmas, there is a chance for the unintended one (*cherry*) to be accidentally selected. ...

Example (2) also involves a semantic relation: *high* and *low* are antonyms. Antonyms and other semantic oppositions in fact form the most frequent type of word substitution. Their causa-tion may be similar to the above case, but there is an additional feature. *High* and *low* are strong associates (stronger than *grape* and *cherry*). ...

Example (3) has a different etiology. The speaker intended to say *Get out of the car* to someone but that moment glanced up at a storefront with the word *Clark's* printed on it. Then *clark* intruded, creating an environmental contamination (Garrett 1980). There was no conceptual spreading of activation from CAR to CLARK. Rather, the printed word Clark seems to have activated the corresponding lemma.

Example (4) has a still different cause. It appears that *branch* may have activated its associate *tree*, allowing the lemma *tree* to be selected instead of the target lemma *roof*. Again it is unclear whether activation spread at the conceptual level (from BRANCH to TREE), at the lemma level (from *roof* to *tree*) or both. Was the speaker really thinking of a tree when the error occurred? We will never know.

▷ *What do you think the authors mean when they say that* 'high *and* low *are strong associates' and that* branch *is an associate of* tree? *How is this notion related to the 'Freudian slip', as discussed on pages 32–3?*

▷ *The authors mention two other types of error: blends and exchanges. Which do you think the following are examples of:*

   Seymour sliced the knife with a salami.
   The competition is a little stougher.

   Do you think the Spoonerisms mentioned on page 32 belong to either of these types?

Text 11

HERBERT CLARK and EVE CLARK: *Psychology and Language: An Introduction to Psycholinguistics.* Harcourt Brace Jovanovich 1977, page 225.

It is easy, and common, to assume that speaking and listening, like reading and writing, are closely related and simply reverse processes of each other. This text makes the point that the relationship between production and reception processes is not so straightforward.

One word of caution. It is easy to fall into the trap of thinking that speaking is simply listening in reverse. In speaking, meaning is turned into sounds, and in listening, sounds are turned into meaning. The parallels are there, of course, but the differences are much more striking. At the sound end, speaking requires the motor activation of the speech organs, while listening consists of an auditory analysis of the speech signal. These two activities involve different organs—the mouth versus the ear—and distinct mental faculties—motor activation versus auditory analysis. At the meaning end, speakers begin with the intention of affecting listeners and turn this intention into a plan of an utterance; at the other end, listeners recognize the speakers' plan and infer their intentions. Again, these two activities are quite distinct … The illusion of similarity is engendered by the fact that speaking and listening both deal with the same structural units: phonetic segments, words, constituents, sentences, speech acts, and discourse structure. But just because speaking and listening have a medium in common, they need not involve similar processes. The tools, skills, materials, and procedures used in speaking are plainly different from those used in listening.

▷ How does this passage suggest an explanation as to why, in learning a foreign language, the ability to comprehend tends to outstrip the ability to speak?

▷ Although these two linguistic processes differ, there are at least some ways in which speaking depends on listening. For example, how is the simultaneous auditory feedback of our articulation useful in speech production?

Chapter 4
Comprehension: understanding what we hear and read

Text 12
PHILIP LIEBERMAN: *Uniquely Human: The Evolution of Speech, Thought, and Selfless Behavior.* Harvard University Press 1991, pages 46–7.

Comprehension begins with the perception of sounds, and Lieberman demonstrates the complexity of this process by describing how speech sounds are acoustically produced by the vocal tract. The resonance of the human voice is measured by acoustic units called formant frequencies.

We humans perform some other remarkable feats as we listen to speech. We have to estimate the probable length of a speaker's supralaryngeal airway in order to assign a particular formant frequency pattern to a particular speech sound. Different-length vocal tracts will have different formant frequencies; a short vocal tract will produce speech sounds that have higher formant frequencies than a long vocal tract, just as a piccolo and a bassoon produce musical notes with higher and lower pitches respectively. The length of the supralaryngeal airway differs greatly in humans: in young children it is half as long as in adults. Adults' vocal tracts also vary in length, and because of this variation there is overlap between the formant frequency patterns that convey different speech sounds. If we interpreted the formant sounds of speech like the notes produced by woodwind instruments, the speech sounds of people with different vocal tract lengths would not have the same phonetic value. For example, the word *bit* spoken by a large adult male speaker can have the same formant frequency pattern as the word *bet* produced by a smaller male. Yet we 'hear' the large person's *bit* as *bit* rather than as *bet*.

▷ *How do these anatomical differences account for the initial difficulty we often encounter understanding the speech of someone we are meeting for the first time, or are hearing for the first time on the telephone?*

▷ *Lieberman likens the sounds of human voices to the different sounds musical instruments make, but in what ways is listening to speech more complex and difficult than listening to instrumental music?*

Text 13

GRACE YEMI-KOMSHIAN: 'Speech perception' in Jean Gleason and Nan Ratner (eds.): *Psycholinguistics*. Harcourt, Brace, Jovanovich 1993, pages 92–3

Speech characteristically consists of an unbroken stream of sounds. Yemi-Komshian describes the complex process of analysing this stream into meaningful units.

Unlike print, speech does not contain cues for the beginning and end of words or of individual speech units, which we will call *phonetic segments*. When we speak, our articulatory gestures are smooth and continuous. If we were to write speech as it actually sounds, we might transcribe our lecture notes as follows: *Spokenwordsarenotseparatedbyspaceslikewordsareinprint.*
Notice that is difficult to read such a sentence because it is less obvious when words end and new words begin.

Even though it is relatively easy for us to segment speech, we should remember that phonetic segments are not like beads strung on a string, one segment after another. Rather, it is better to compare speech to a braid, in which the properties which help us identify phonetic segments are tightly intertwined and overlap greatly. One of the great challenges for speech perception researchers is to determine how individual sounds are isolated (segmented) from the complex speech signal, and how they are identified appropriately.

▷ *Following Yemi-Komshian's metaphor, what are some reasons why written words are more like beads on a string but spoken words seem to be braided together?*

Text 14

MICHAEL GARMAN: *Psycholinguistics*. Cambridge University Press 1990, page 315

As explained in Section 1, one proposal for accounting for comprehension difficulty was to equate it with the grammatical complexity of the sentence being processed (the so-called derivational theory of complexity). But, as this passage points out, other strategies have been subsequently proposed.

Bever suggested that the listener tests an input sequence for the goodness of fit it offers with certain canonical schemas such as 'Actor ... Action ... (Object)'. Word strings that readily yield to this sort of analysis are predicted to be easier to process than those that do not; for these latter, the processing system has to refer to further canonical schemas in order to determine their status. This suggests a hierarchy of canonical schemas, with those at the top being the ones that are most often required in the language, and those towards the bottom serving as fall-back devices, used only when necessary. The virtue of this approach is that it provides for a characterisation of how easy or difficult it is for the listener to process an utterance, independently of the terms in which the utterance may have been produced by the speaker. Thus, in the example

The horse raced past the barn fell

we can say that the construction is, from one point of view, a restricted subject–relative clause type, with passivisation of the relative clause and deletion of the optional relative pronoun and passive auxiliary verb (*the horse (that was) raced past* ...). But we may also note that, from the listener's viewpoint it presents peculiar difficulties, because of the high-priority canonical schema that powerfully operates to treat the initial sequence *the horse raced past the barn* ... as 'Actor ... Action ... Modifier', in the main clause of the construction. This, furthermore, appears to represent fairly directly what people report after hearing this construction; there is a feeling of suddenly being stranded when the word *fell* is reached, since it is not catered for in terms of the analysis applied up to this point. There is a sensation also of being forced back to re-analyze the initial sequence, this time equipped with the knowledge that *fell* occurs where it does.

This sort of phenomenon is known, picturesquely, as a *garden path effect.* ...

▷ *Garman refers to the influence of canonical schemas (i.e. established patterns of conceptualization) on comprehension. How would you account for the following by reference to the notion of canonical schema described here?: The waiter brought the wine was drunk.*

▷ *In Text 10, mention is made of the association between words. How do you think this notion is relevant to the ideas about sentence processing in this text?*

Text 15

JANET FODOR: 'Comprehending sentence structure' in Lila Gleitman and Mark Liberman (eds.): *Language: An Invitation to Cognitive Science.* The MIT Press 1995, page 213

The language we produce is full of grammatical gaps, although we are almost entirely unaware of them. Fodor describes the psycholinguistic relevance of these 'empty categories'.

These non-overt constituents are what linguists call *empty categories (ECs).* They are *categories* in the syntactican's sense; that is, they are noun phrases or verbs or relative pronouns, and so forth. They are *empty* in the sense of lacking any phonological (or orthographic) realization. Thus, an empty category is a piece of the sentence structure, but it is not pronounced (or written) by the sentence producer, so it is not audible (or visible) to the sentence perceiver. The perceiver must deduce both its existence and its properties. An example is the 'missing' verb *flew* in the second clause of sentence (7).

(7) John flew to Paris, and Mary to Chicago.

Mary is a noun phrase (NP) and *to Chicago* is a prepositional phrase (PP). A clause cannot normally consist of just an NP followed by a PP; it must have a verb. It seems reasonable to suppose, then, that the structure of (7) is (8), where there is a verb in both clauses in accord with general structural principles, but where the second verb is phonologically empty.

(8) John flew to Paris, and Mary (flew) to Chicago.

▷ *Fodor points out that ECs are 'empty' in that they are not pronounced or written, but are they also 'empty' of grammatical meaning?*

▷ *What advantage do ECs provide for the listeners and speakers of a language?*

Text 16

LAWRENCE BARSALOU: *Cognitive Psychology: An Overview for Cognitive Scientists.* Lawrence Earlbaum Associates 1992, pages 262–3

We often imply meanings that we do not explicitly state. Barsalou explains one of the ways in which implied meaning differs from literal meaning.

Is it always necessary to compute a sentence's literal meaning prior to computing its implied meaning? Some studies have found that people skip computing the literal meaning, because the context generates such a strong expectancy about the implied meaning. Imagine that someone at dinner is watching you use the pepper grinder and then utters when you're finished:

Can you pass the pepper?

In this context, the literal question about your ability to pass the pepper is bypassed, because the intended request is so salient. As this example illustrates, many indirect requests are idiomatic. Given the frequent cooccurrence of their surface form and implied meaning, it is not surprising that people activate the implied meaning automatically. …

People do not always ignore literal meaning, however. Imagine that someone calls a merchant on the telephone and asks:

Would you mind telling me what time you close tonight?

The merchant could provide two kinds of information in response: First, she could respond to the literal question and state whether she minds providing the information. Second, she could respond to the indirect request and state what time her business closes. If she bypasses the literal meaning and only processes the intended message, then she should not begin her utterance by saying 'yes' or 'no' in response to the literal question. Instead, she should only provide the closing time. If she also processes the literal meaning, though, she may preface the closing time by stating whether she minds providing it. To test this, H. H. Clark (1979) had a research assistant call local merchants and ask them their closing times. He found that the merchants often responded to the literal meaning of the request, as well as to the indirect request (for example 'No, 10 o'clock'). Whether they compute both the literal and implied meaning of a sentence, or whether they only compute the implied meaning, depends on current circumstances and the nature of the utterance.

▷ What are some of the conditions necessary for people to comprehend the implied meaning of 'Can you pass the pepper?'

▷ Imagine you are the merchant being questioned in this survey. What other answers could you give? What implications would the caller draw from these other responses?

▷ Why do people often use 'implied' questions in communication and not rely solely on 'literal' ones?

Chapter 5
Dissolution: language loss

Text 17
DONALD FOSS and DAVID HAKES: *Psycholinguistics: An Introduction to the Psychology of Language*. Prentice-Hall 1978, pages 215–16

Foss and Hakes demonstrate the importance of self-monitoring in speech production by describing an experiment where disruptions in normal monitoring can induce stuttering in fluent speakers.

It is generally found, for example, that hearing another speaker's voice after a delay does not have as much disruptive effect as hearing one's own voice. And Webster and his colleagues ... have found evidence suggesting that auditory feedback [hearing an amplified recording of one's own voice] affects the timing control of articulatory gestures even if it does not affect what those gestures are. They have shown that for stutterers delaying auditory feedback actually decreases the amount of stuttering, an effect exactly the opposite of that found with non-stuttering normal speakers. In accounting for this, Webster suggested that a part of the problem for stutterers is that their speech perception mechanisms are defective. For them, normal feedback has the same kind of disruptive effect that delayed feedback has on normal speakers. If this is the case, it implies that auditory feedback is used by normal speakers, perhaps in maintaining the rhythmic fluency of their speech.

▷ Why are feedback loops important in normal language production? What communicative problems do you think you would have if you experienced delayed feedback?

Text 18

HAROLD GOODGLASS and EDITH KAPLAN: *The Assessment of Aphasia and Related Disorders.* Lea and Febinger 1972, pages 10–11

Most aphasic patients lose the ability to write, probably, as Goodglass and Kaplan acknowledge, because writing involves so many other language sub-skills.

Writing is the most complex of the language modalities and has a correspondingly large number of dimensions for examination. At the level or mere motor execution, writing may fail with respect to the recall of the form of letters or of the movements involved in producing them. As in speech, there are automatized, serial tasks such as one's name and address, or the alphabet, which may be preserved when all other writing is lost. Slavish copying from a printed model may still be possible when the subject cannot transcribe into cursive script ...

When a word is written to dictation, we do not know whether the process involved is primarily one of phonetic translation from sound to spelling or whether comprehension of the meaning of the word has played an intermediary role. However, when the patient is required to write the names of pictured objects, we know that the initiating process is the concept of the object and we are testing 'written word-finding.' Observation of the writing process and of patient's errors indicate that three types of association are at work. One is the automatic translation of sounds into the motor sequences for letters, following the phonic rules of the language; another is the recall of syllables and short words as complete graphic motor sequences, bolstered by a visual model of the word configurations; a third is the availability of oral spelling as a guide to writing. Because oral spelling is unhampered by the slowness of recalling and writing individual letters, we often find oral spelling a bit superior to written spelling [and] to dictation. Only by specifically testing each process do we obtain an inkling as to how they are interacting in the patient's performance of a complex writing task.

▷ *As elaborated in this text, even simple writing tasks involve a variety of skills. According to the authors, what are three or four skills a writer must possess simply to write down a single, dictated word?*

▷ *Even brain-damaged patients can frequently write their signature. What are some implications of this for understanding how the brain controls written language?*

Text 19

DAVID CARROLL: *Psychology of Language.* Brooks/Cole Publishing Company 1994, pages 345–6.

As explained in the following passage, damage in Broca's area leads specifically to deficiencies in speech production.

The disorder BROCA'S APHASIA, also known as EXPRESSIVE APHASIA, was discovered by and named after the French surgeon Paul Broca. Broca studied individuals who, after a stroke or accident, displayed halting, agrammatic speech. These individuals were often unable to express themselves by more than a single word at a time. Moreover, some parts of their speech were more affected than others: content words such as nouns and verbs were usually well preserved, whereas function words such as adjectives and articles were not. ...

The clear difficulty in articulating speech by Broca's aphasics might lead us to believe its agrammatic nature is due to a voluntary economy of effort. That is, since articulation is so difficult—they speak slowly and often confuse related sounds—perhaps Broca's aphasics are trying to save effort by expressing only the most important words. Although this factor may have some role in the disorder, it is not the most important feature since many Broca's aphasics do no better after repeated self-correction. Moreover, the writing of these patients is usually at least as impaired as their speech, and individual words of grammatical context are spared. These considerations suggest that the main feature of this disorder is the loss of the ability to express grammatical relationships, either in speech or in writing.

▷ *Reflecting back on some of the slips-of-the-tongue examples in Chapter 3, what are some of the ways aphasic speech differs from the mistakes made in 'normal' spoken language?*

▷ *What are the arguments Carroll musters to support the notion that Broca's aphasia is due to the dissolution of grammar?*

Text 20

MACDONALD CRITCHLEY: *The Divine Banquet of the Brain and Other Essays.* Raven Press 1979, pages 56–7

Despite their linguistic impairment, all aphasics appear to be clear in their semantic intentions. This final excerpt, cited by Critchley, is from a letter written by a schizophrenic. In marked contrast to the attempts by aphasics to communicate, although the semantic intentions are unclear there are only slight signs of linguistic impairment.

... I like Titbits weekly. I like Titbits weekly too. I should like Titbits ordered weekly. I need jam, golden syrup or treacle, sugar. I fancy ham sandwiches and pork pies. Cook me a pork pie and I fancy sausage rools I want ham sandwiches. I want tomatoes and pickles and salt and sandwiches of corn beef and sandwiches of milk loaf and cucumber sandwiches. I want plain biscuits buttered, rusks, and cheese biscuits I want bread and cheese.

I want Swiss roll and plain cake, I want pastries, jam tarts. I should like some of your pie you have for second course, some pastry. I want biscuits, fancy biscuits and fancy cakes. I want sweets, bulls-eyes or cloves. I want rissols. I want rissols. I fancy fruit, do bring some oranges, apples, bananas, pears. Do brong some fruit, I get dry oranges. I got tea for all next week from March 10th Sunday, all the week till Sunday March 17th. I shall want more tea Sunday, March 17th, the following week after March 17th Sunday. I want sugar I want jam, golden-syrup or treacle. I like plum jam. I like butter. It would be a treat. ...

▷ *Ignoring this writer's obvious lack of coherence for the moment, note that she actually displays a great deal of linguistic knowledge. Do you think this person is a native speaker of English? What are a few grammar rules she obviously knows? What do you notice about her vocabulary?*

▷ *What evidence can you find to support the claim that the language of schizophrenics is less a linguistic impairment and more a cognitive or psychological disability?*

SECTION 3
References

The references which follow can be classified into introductory level (marked ■□□), more advanced and consequently more technical (marked ■■□), and specialized, very demanding (marked ■■■).

Chapter 1
Introduction

■■□

DAVID CARROLL: *Psychology of Language.* Brooks/Cole Publishing 1994

A fully updated revision of an earlier edition, this well-organized survey of psycholinguistics provides comprehensive coverage of all the traditional domains of the field. The book is written in a clear and balanced manner and contains relevant graphs, tables, and illustrations which help explicate the experiments which are reviewed.

■■■

MICHAEL FORRESTER: *Psychology of Language: A Critical Introduction.* Sage Publications 1996

An unusual approach to psycholinguistics in that the author approaches the field via literary and social criticism. Discussion of experimental evidence is absent, replaced, instead, by attention to the analysis of signs, symbols, and conversation and to competing approaches to the relationship between language, thought, and society.

■■□

MICHAEL GARMAN: *Psycholinguistics*.
Cambridge University Press 1990

A very thorough, carefully written, and fully documented survey of the whole field of psycholinguistics, with separate chapters on each of the topics dealt with in Section 1 of this present book.

■■■

MORTON ANN GERNSBACHER (ed.): *Handbook of Psycholinguistics*. Academic Press 1994

This is a comprehensive compendium of essays by authorities in the field on all aspects of psycholinguistics. It is encyclopedic in coverage and, as a work of reference, represents a complete account of the current state of the art, including a final chapter on future directions of inquiry.

■■□

JEAN GLEASON and NAN RATNER (eds.): *Psycholinguistics*.
Harcourt Brace Jovanovich 1993

Ratner and Gleason's introductory chapter to this informative anthology edited by the same two authors is a succinct yet comprehensive description of the main concepts and themes found in the psychology of language.

■■□

JOSEPH KESS: *Psycholinguistics: Psychology, Linguistics, and the Study of Natural Language*. John Benjamins 1992

A traditional and readable survey of the field with an unusually comprehensive coverage of syntax and discourse analysis. Also exceptional is an opening chapter on the history of psycholinguistics, but missing are tables, figures, and illustrations to amplify the text.

■□□

DANNY STEINBERG: *An Introduction to Psycholinguistics*.
Longman 1993

An attractively illustrated and highly readable introduction to a wide range of relevant topics (for example animal language, the 'wild children', sign language, and the Sapir-Whorf hypothesis). The author is quick to express strong opinions on a variety of topics, and except for an unnecessary and confusing digression critiquing some of Chomsky's views in Chapter 6, the book challenges the reader with its refreshingly assertive and non-academic style.

■■□

INSUP TAYLOR and M. MARTIN TAYLOR:
Psycholinguistics: Learning and Using Language.
Prentice-Hall 1990

A meticulously referenced survey with many different topics cited and illustrated. Because of this, the volume might serve better as a reference book than a text. Since the first and senior author is a non-native speaker of English, the book provides several perspectives on second language acquisition not normally found in psycholinguistic textbooks.

Chapter 2
Acquisition: when I was a child, I spoke as a child

■■□

DEREK BICKERTON: *Language and Species.*
University of Chicago 1992

This fascinating book deals with the evolution of human language, arguing that child language acquisition along with pidgins and creoles (the author's specialty) are 'living linguistic fossils' which provide evidence for the nature and evolution of speech in human history. Like many other psycholinguists, the author musters strong evidence for discontinuity between human and animal communication.

■■■

PAUL BLOOM (ed.): *Language Acquisition: Core Readings.*
MIT Press 1994

This large anthology contains 18 chapters on topics ranging from the effect of mothers' voices on infant learning to the manner in which blind babies pick up speech. Most of the contributions are quite technical and narrow in scope, but they all pertain to the debate over whether nature or nurture is most influential in shaping language development.

■■□

RAY JACKENDOFF: *Patterns in the Mind: Language and Human Nature*. Basic Books 1994

This volume discusses many different topics which touch on the psychology of language, though much of it focuses on the way children acquire language and how this acquisition supports the notion of universal grammar. There is a brief discussion of music and language, a topic on which the author possesses both personal and professional expertise.

■□□

SHARON JAMES: *Normal Language Acquisition*. College-Hill Press 1990

A short and simple introduction to first language learning which is particularly clear in summarizing the evidence for various stages of syntactic development. Unfortunately, the discussion of competing theories of language acquisition in the final chapter is not satisfactory.

■■□

ANN M. PETERS: *The Units of Language Acquisition*. Cambridge University Press 1983

The basic theme of this book is the way children acquire language by first accumulating formulaic units or prefabricated patterns. Peters shows that their strategies of development do not correspond with descriptive procedures of linguistic analysis.

■□□

STEVEN PINKER: *The Language Instinct*. Harper Perennial 1994

This highly entertaining and popular book serves as a general introduction to linguistics, but much of it deals with psycholinguistic issues. The author cites compelling and consistent evidence to support his contention that language acquisition takes place largely because of the innate influence of universal grammar.

■□□

PETER REICH: *Language Development*. Prentice-Hall 1986

Although this introduction to child language acquisition has been available for more than a decade, it remains one of the most complete and readable introductions to this field. Well-illustrated by tables, figures, prose inserts, and cartoons, the book is also well-written in a personal yet authoritative style. It includes chapters on bilingualism and child language disabilities, and also a copious list of references at the end.

Chapter 3
Production: putting words in one's mouth

■■□

JEAN GLEASON and NAN RATNER (eds.): *Psycholinguistics*. Harcourt Brace Jovanovich 1993

Victoria Fromkin's chapter, 'Speech production', is a well-illustrated introduction to the formulation stage of speech production. The author was a pioneer in the use of slips of the tongue as data for psycholinguistic research, and speech errors and models of production are especially well-covered in this essay.

■■■

LILA GLEITMAN and MARK LIBERMAN (eds.): *Language: An Invitation to Cognitive Science, Volume 1*. MIT Press 1995

This book contains 14 chapters. All of them are fairly short but most of them demand careful reading. Several of the contributions deal directly or indirectly with the production of speech and language.

■■□

DAVID MCNEILL: *Psycholinguistics: A New Approach*. Harper & Row 1987

This book is difficult to read and somewhat uneven in the way topics are covered, but, as promised in the title, the author offers a creative explanation of speech production. The lengthy Chapter 5 can be read independently in order to understand the author's convincing contention that 'imagistic' communication is packaged along with speech and is manifested by the gestures and body language we use as we converse.

Chapter 4
Comprehension: understanding what we hear and read

■■■

LAWRENCE BARSALOU: *Cognitive Psychology: An Overview for Cognitive Scientists.* Lawrence Erlbaum 1992

Though this book does not deal directly with the field of psycholinguistics, it is germane to the topic of language comprehension since it deals in some detail with psychologists' attempt to define and explain the way in which we contextualize new information into our 'frames' or pre-conditioned expectations.

■■□

JEAN GLEASON and NAN RATNER (eds.): *Psycholinguistics.* Harcourt Brace Jovanovich 1993

In their chapter 'Words and meanings: From primitives to complex organization', Kathy Hirsh-Pasek and Lauretta Reeves present a brief review of the psycholinguistic research on morphological recognition followed by a lengthy, up-to-date, and balanced survey of many different models which psycholinguists have posited to account for lexical comprehension and semantic processing.

In his chapter on 'Sentence processing', Arthur Wingfield covers the comprehension of clauses and sentences by discussing the roles of ambiguity, prosody, semantics, predictability, and memory in the way native speakers process syntactic information.

■■■

VIVIEN TARTTER: *Language Processes.* Holt, Rinehart & Winston 1986

This lengthy and rather technical introduction to psycholinguistics deals with a wide range of topics, but it is particularly informative and insightful in its analysis of speech perception. Chapters 6 and 7 detail the acoustics and the psychology of how people hear disparate sounds as discrete phonemes and also present arguments for and against the various models which have been proposed for speech perception.

Chapter 5
Dissolution: language loss

■■□

JEAN GLEASON and NAN RATNER (eds.): *Psycholinguistics.* Harcourt Brace Jovanovich 1993

William Dingwall's chapter on neurolinguistics, 'The biological bases of human communicative behavior', is a well-written and superbly illustrated introduction to the neuroanatomy of speech. The author elaborates on contemporary methods of measuring brain functions and demonstrates how these measures are used to corroborate neurolinguistic hypotheses.

■■□

PHILIP LIEBERMAN: *Uniquely Human: The Evolution of Speech, Thought, and Selfless Behavior.* Harvard University 1991

This is a wide-ranging discussion of the origin and evolution of human speech. It includes topics such as aphasia, neurolinguistic processing, the evolution of the 'organs of speech,' speech perception, and the effects of culture on altruistic behavior.

■■□

HERBERT SELIGER and ROBERT VAGO (eds.): *First Language Attrition.* Cambridge 1991

This anthology is devoted to language loss in bilinguals. The 16 contributions are divided into three sections: Survey studies, Group studies, and Investigations of individual cases. Together, these contributions examine 10 languages, most of them lost because of contact with English.

SECTION 4
Glossary

Alzheimer's disease A progressive degeneration of the brain which results, among other things, in the general dissolution of memory, cognition, and language. [86]

American Sign Language (ASL) A language used by the deaf or hearing impaired in the United States. It is based on manual and facial movements. [15]

aphasia The dissolution of language and speech caused by damage to the brain, most typically, in the central area of the left hemisphere: cf. **Broca's aphasia** and **Wernicke's aphasia**. [73]

aphasiology The study of the verbal behavior of aphasics in an attempt to better understand the ways in which the brain processes and produces language. [76]

articulation The third stage of speech production, after the words and phrases have been conceptualized and formulated. At this stage they are translated into the sounds and syllables of actual speech. [27]

autism A disease, the causes of which are unknown, that is manifested in infancy and characterized by extreme asocial behavior and the absence of normal language acquisition. [83]

Automated Transition Networks (ATNs) A model of neurolinguistics which claims that much of language is produced by means of chains of associated words. [65]

autonomic The part of the nervous system that automatically controls the body functions necessary for life, and thus areas of the brain not directly responsible for language and speech. [8]

babbling Strings of consonant–vowel syllable clusters produced by infants. Emerging during the second six months of a baby's life, this stage of language production is the first indication that an infant is actually learning sounds in its mother tongue. *See also* **canonical** and **marginal babbling**. [10]

bathtub effect The tendency to remember the beginnings and ends of words better than the middle portions. [57]

Broca's aphasia Also called motor or expressive aphasia, this is the loss of the ability to produce words or speak fluently as a result of damage to **Broca's area**: cf. **Wernicke's aphasia**. [74]

Broca's area The lower portion of the motor cortex of the brain (just above the left ear, in front of **Wernicke's area**) which is responsible for the production of words and sentences: cf. **Wernicke's area**. [73]

canalization The laying down of neural pathways in the young brain in response to repeated exposure and practice (e.g. the neurological basis for the ability of children to produce the sounds of their mother tongue accurately). [76]

canonical babbling The repetition of syllables by infants beginning at about eight months of age which first shows that they are acquiring distinct features of the mother tongue, e.g. Chinese babies begin to babble with tones: cf. **marginal babbling**. [10]

categorical perception Listening to a stream of speech and automatically dividing this continuous flow of sound into the phonemes of the listener's native language. [54]

coarticulation The assimilation of phonemes into those which immediately precede or follow them in the stream of speech, thus distorting their normal articulation and making identification difficult. [44]

competence Implicit knowledge we have about the language(s) we speak, e.g. we can easily identify an ungrammatical sentence even though we may not be able to describe what rule(s) it violates: cf. **performance**. [47]

conceptualization The first and most abstract stage of speech production where the speaker makes the decisions about how to frame an idea into language. [27]

cooing In contrast to crying, infants at this early stage of oral production express 'coos' of contentment which are precursors to babbling. [10]

corpus callosum A wide sheath of association pathways which serves to transmit information between the two cerebral hemispheres, making it almost impossible, in the normal brain, for one hemisphere to store data inaccessible to the other. [71]

creative construction Concerns the tendency of young children acquiring their mother tongue to come up with overgeneralizations about the language which they have never been exposed to (e.g. 'I'm hicking up!'). [20]

critical period Hypothetically, approximately the first ten years of life. Some linguists believe that certain aspects of language acquisition (e.g. sounding like a native speaker) can never be fully acquired if they have not been learned during this time. [22]

Derivational Theory of Complexity (DTC) A now discredited theory that the psycholinguistic difficulty of a sentence, as measured by memory load or processing time, is directly proportional to the number of grammatical rules contained in that utterance. [60]

developmental psycholinguistics The examination of how infants and children acquire the ability to comprehend and speak their mother tongue. [7]

diachronic Studying linguistic change over time in contrast to looking at language as it is used at a given moment: cf. **synchronic**. [5]

Down's syndrome An inherited disease which often results in significant loss of cognitive processing capacity, but which does not inhibit language acquisition to a corresponding degree. [84]

egocentric speech A term used by Piaget and others to characterize the way the language of young children appears both to reflect and shape their early thinking. [12]

equipotential The neurological notion that, especially in young brains, most areas of the cerebral cortex are free to be programmed for the processing of a wide range of cognitive or linguistic functions. [73]

errors The production of incorrect forms in speech or writing by a non-native speaker of a second language, the result of incomplete knowledge of the rules of that target language: cf. **mistakes**. [46]

feedback loop The sensory information the body provides during the production of speech which allows the speaker to monitor and adjust the articulation of individual sounds and words. [47]

formulation The second stage of speech production, after conceptualization, when the message is framed into words, phrases, and clauses by the speaker. [27]

garden-pathing The phenomenon in the comprehension of sentences that the sequence of words tends to create in us a certain expectation about their meaning. This may or may not be confirmed by the remainder of the sentence. [65]

hemispherectomy The surgical removal of either the left or right hemisphere of the brain of a child as an extreme measure against a life-threatening illness or neurological condition. [76]

holophrastic Term used to describe one-word sentences used by small children but also found in adult speech (e.g. 'Milk?' 'Here!'). [13]

iconic One-to-one relationships between signs and their referents (e.g. lowering the pitch of your voice on 'deep' when you describe someone by saying he 'speaks in a *deep* voice'): cf. **symbolic**. [9]

idiomorphs Words small children invent in their initial attempts to acquire a language (e.g. 'wa wa' for 'cat'). [11]

imagistic thinking The visual component of the conceptualization of language that is ultimately manifested in the gestures which accompany speech: cf. **syntactic thinking**. [27]

innateness The theory that ascribes a major part of language learning to genetically packaged knowledge which is then triggered, after birth, by exposure to large amounts of linguistic input: *See* **Language Acquisition Device** and **Universal Grammar**. [17]

Johnson theory The behaviorally-based explanation for stuttering which claims it is largely caused by the undue attention paid by parents and/or teachers to a child with the aim of encouraging correct articulation: cf. **Orton/Travis theory**. [81]

Language Acquisition Device (LAD) According to Chomsky, the innate mental mechanism designed uniquely for the acquisition of language. *See* **innateness** and **Universal Grammar**. [18]

logogen The cumulative information we store about a word we are comprehending, and which we use to guess its meaning. [56]

Long Term Memory (LTM) Memory as we normally think of it, whether it is of an event from childhood or of the name of a person we have just met: cf. **Short Term Memory (STM)**. [85]

marginal babbling An infant's initial attempts to produce syllables, usually beginning at the age of about six months: cf. **canonical babbling**. [10]

Mean Length of Utterance (MLU) The average number of morphemes an infant produces in its utterances. Researchers use this as a measure of the complexity of a child's early speech production. [24]

mentalistic Relying on logic and intuition rather than directly observable experimental evidence to support a hypothesis. [32]

mistakes The production of incorrect forms in speech or writing, the result of factors such as carelessness or fatigue. All speakers make mistakes, whether they are native or non-native users of the target language: cf. **errors**. [46]

mnemonists People with super-normal abilities to remember large amounts of information (e.g. someone who can recite an entire play or book from memory). [66]

modular Independent from other forms of cognition—the belief that language acquisition is greatly facilitated by a special faculty of the human mind uniquely designed for language and speech. [54]

morphology The study of the structure of words or the structural patterns of the words in any particular language. [36]

motor cortex A small vertical strip of brain roughly in the mid portion of both hemispheres which is primarily responsible for initiating complex muscular movement, as in the articulation of speech sounds: cf. **sensory cortex**. [72]

neurolinguistics The branch of psycholinguistics which investigates the the use of language in experimental or clinical conditions as a window to the way in which the brain produces and processes linguistic information. [71]

neuroplasticity The capacity of a young child's brain to allocate different areas of the cortex for complex human behaviors such as language. [76]

Orton/Travis theory An innatist explanation for stuttering that claims that genetic, not environmental, factors are primarily responsible for this disability: cf. **Johnson theory**. [81]

Parallel Distributed Processings (PDP) A model of cognition that attempts to account for complex behaviors such as the processing and production of speech by positing the existence of completely separate but concurrent and parallel cognitive systems operating at the same time. [55]

performance Words actually spoken and written: the explicit, physical manifestation of our intuitive linguistic competence: cf. **competence**. [47]

phoneme monitoring A task used in experiments. Subjects are asked to listen to a sentence and to press a button as soon as they hear a certain sound (e.g. /p/). Their reaction time is a direct measure of the complexity of the sentence. [63]

phoneme restoration effect A device employed by psycholinguists to investigate comprehension; e.g. subjects hear 'ail' in a paragraph describing how water is gathered and believe they heard the word 'pail'. [51]

phrase structure rules The syntactic skeleton of a sentence which specifies all the major constituents which must be accounted for in that particular utterance, e.g. 'The kitten drank the milk' can be subdivided into a noun phrase ('the kitten') and a verb phrase ('drank the milk'). [16, 59]

pivot Word used by young children either to begin or end a two-word utterance (e.g. 'Hi Mommy', 'Hi Kitty', or 'Milk allgone', 'Mommy allgone'). [15]

Positron Emission Tomography (PET) The use of a mildly radioactive dye in the blood to measure the flow of blood in a patient's brain. This can reveal the way neurological disorders such as tumors can affect the way the brain programs speaking or listening. [45]

pragmatics The study of what people mean when they use language in normal social interaction. [38]

priming Covertly eliciting a certain word in a psycholinguistic experiment (e.g. in a listening task, 'right' might be primed in a text about street directions; 'write' might be primed in a text which describes the importance of literacy). [31]

psycholinguistics The study of the normal and abnormal use of language and speech to gain a better understanding of how the human mind functions: cf. **psychology of language**. [4]

psychologically real Description of the way in which the structures and categories of a particular language appears to affect a person's ability to process linguistic information. [34]

psychology of language A synonym for **psycholinguistics**. [4]

rate The amount of time it takes children to learn a specific sound, structure, or specified number of words. Language acquisition rates vary a great deal among very young children. *See* **stage**. [22]

resonance The combined harmonics made by the vocal tract in the articulation of any speech sound. [43]

schematic knowledge Specific information which we bring to any new situation based on our accumulated experience with similar situations. [58]

Second Language Acquisition (SLA) The study of how people acquire an additional language, often by means of an analysis of the errors they make. [46]

segmental phonemes Vowels and consonants: sounds which are relatively easy to divide into individual units of sound: cf. **suprasegmental**. [10]

self-monitoring The fourth and final stage of speech production, after conceptualization, formulation, and articulation, when we edit our message and correct any errors. [27]

sensory cortex The narrow strip of brain parallel to the motor cortex which is primarily responsible for the processing of all sensory information to the brain and which controls our ability to comprehend speech: cf. **motor cortex**. [72]

Short Term Memory (STM) Also called working memory. Our very limited ability to remember new information without storing it in **Long Term Memory**: cf. **Long Term Memory (LTM)**. [86]

slips of the tongue Mistakes in speech (or in writing) which provide psycholinguistic evidence for the way we formulate words and phrases: cf. **Spoonerisms**. [30]

sociolinguistics In its larger sense, the study of language and society, or, more narrowly, how social factors influence linguistic structure and use. [38]

split-brain operation Rarely performed surgery where the corpus callosum is either partially or entirely severed to spare a patient from severe epileptic seizures. It can create unusual neuropsychological constraints. [77]

Spoonerisms Slips of the tongue which create new phrases with often unintended or humorous meanings (e.g. 'the breast in bed' instead of 'the best in bread'): cf. **slips of the tongue**. [32]

spreading activation networks The neurolinguistic model which posits that repeated use of certain words or phrases in the same context will create neuronal networks that facilitate rapid recognition or production of these words. [58]

stage Irrespective of their rate of language acquisition, all children appear to progress through the same stages or sequences of development (e.g. English-speaking children say 'Why Mommy is leaving now?' before they produce the correct 'Why is Mommy leaving now?'). *See* **rate**. [15]

suprasegmental Features of speech beyond the individual sound such as pitch, stress, rhythm, and intonation: cf. **segmental phonemes**. [11]

symbolic Signs which have a random and arbitary relationship with their referents (e.g. 'sun' is a small word but a large object; 'micro-organism' is a large word but a tiny object): cf. **iconic**. [9]

synchronic Studying language and speech as they are used at a given moment and not in terms of how they have evolved over time: cf. **diachronic**. [6]

syntactic thinking Thinking in words in a linear, sequential manner: cf. **imagistic thinking**. [27]

Tip-Of-the-Tongue (TOT) A phenomenon we experience when trying to retrieve a word we know we know, but are still unable to recall at that moment. [56]

Transformational-Generative (TG) grammar Chomsky's model of grammar which posits a set of grammatical rules, or 'transformations', which operate on phrase structures to generate all and only the sentences of a language. [14, 59]

tuning Making minor revisions in a hypothesis to accommodate new data (e.g. a child who believes that all past-tense forms end with -ed creates the word 'wented' after hearing 'went' used to indicate past time). [19]

Universal Grammar (UG) An abstract set of rules and principles which govern the syntax of all languages and which many linguists believe to be innately specified in all humans. *See* **innateness** and **Language Acquisition Device**. [18]

Voice Onset Timing (VOT) The brief burst of air which precedes the articulation of all stop consonants, and which provides phonetic information listeners use to distinguish between sounds like /k/ and /g/. [52]

Wernicke's aphasia Loss of the ability to comprehend speech or written language as a result of damage to Wernicke's area of the brain: cf. **Broca's aphasia**. [74]

Wernicke's area The lower portion of the sensory cortex of the brain (just above the left ear, behind **Broca's area**) which is responsible for the processing of most speech and language: cf. **Broca's area**. [73]

Acknowledgements

The author and publisher are grateful to the following for permission to reproduce extracts from copyright material:

Addison Wesley Longman for an extract from Danny Steinberg: *An Introduction to Psycholinguistics* (1993).

Cambridge University Press for extracts from Ann M. Peters: *The Units of Language Acquisition* (1983), and Michael Garman: *Psycholinguistics* (1990).

Lawrence Erlbaum Associates, Inc. for an extract from Lawrence Barsalou: *Cognitive Psychology: An Overview for Cognitive Scientists* (1992).

Jean Berko Gleason for an extract from 'The child's learning of English morphology' in Sol Saporta (ed.): *Psycholinguistics: A Book of Readings* (Holt, Rinehart & Winston 1961), originally published in *Word* 14, 1958.

Harcourt Brace & Company for extracts from Victoria Fromkin: 'Speech production' and Grace Yemi-Komshian: 'Speech Perception', both in Jean Gleason and Nan Ratner (eds.): *Psycholinguistics* (1993), Copyright © 1993 by Holt, Rinehart & Winston; an extract from Herbert Clark and Eve Clark: *Psychology and Language: An Introduction to Psycholinguistics* (1977), Copyright © 1977 by Harcourt Brace & Company; an extract from 'Language production: Grammatical encoding' by Kathryn Block and Willem Levelt in Morton Ann Gernsbacher (ed.): *Handbook of Psycholinguistics* (Academic Press 1994); extracts from 'Language disorders (aphasia)' by H. Goodglass and N. Geschwind in E. C. Carterette and M. P. Friedman (eds):

Handbook of Perception, Volume 7: Language and Speech (Academic Press 1976); an extract from 'Overview: Controversies in language acquisition' by Paul Bloom in *Handbook of Psycholinguistics* (Academic Press 1993) and reprinted in Paul Bloom (ed.): *Language Acquisition: Core Readings* (MIT Press 1994).

Harvard University Press and the Trustees of Amherst College for poem #556 by Emily Dickinson from *The Poems of Emily Dickinson*, edited by Thomas H. Johnson (Cambridge, Mass.: The Belknap Press of Harvard University Press), Copyright © 1951, 1955, 1979, 1983 by the President and Fellows of Harvard College.

Harvard University Press for an extract from Phillip Lieberman: *Uniquely Human: The Evolution of Speech, Thought, and Selfless Behaviour* (Cambridge, Mass.: Harvard University Press), Copyright © 1991 by the President and Fellows of Harvard College.

Alfred A. Knopf, Inc. for an extract from Herbert S. Terrance: *Nim: A Chimpanzee Who Learned Sign Language* (Washington Square Press 1979).

The Linguistic Society of America for an extract from M. D. S. Braine: 'The ontogeny of English phrase structure: The first phrase' in *Language* 39, 1963.

Lippincott-Raven Publishers for an extract from Macdonald Critchley: *The Divine Banquet of the Brain and Other Essays* (Raven 1979).

MIT Press for extracts from Lila Gleitman and Elissa Newport: 'The invention of language by children: Environmental and biological influences on the acquisition of language', and 'Why the child holded the baby rabbits: A case study in language acquisition' by Steven Pinker, both in Daniel Osherson (ed.): *Language: An Introduction to Cognitive Science* (1995); an extract from Janet Fodor: 'Comprehending sentence structure' in Lila Gleitman and Mark Liberman (eds.): *Language: An Invitation to Cognitive Science* (1995).

Oxford University Press, Inc for an extract from 'Human maternal vocalizations to infants as biologically relevant signals: An evolutionary perspective' by Anne Fernald in J. H. Barkow et al: